Paula Heller Garland

second edition

# Living in Consciousness

*Workbook*

## Kendall Hunt
publishing company

All interior images © Shutterstock.com unless otherwise noted.

Cover image © Shutterstock, Inc.

**Kendall Hunt**
publishing company

www.kendallhunt.com
*Send all inquiries to:*
4050 Westmark Drive
Dubuque, IA 52004-1840

Copyright © 2013, 2016 by Kendall Hunt Publishing Company

ISBN 978-1-4652-9782-2

Printed in the United States of America

# Contents

# Introduction

A common thread woven through society, in families, communities, professional settings, academic environments, counseling rooms, and intimate relationships seems to be barriers in communication. Ultimately, *Living in Consciousness* will explore effective communication; however, we will begin with a better understanding of self in order to reach the fullest potential and awareness.

In the workbook section, we will investigate the impact of personal beliefs on relationships with others. Often beliefs are unconsciously defended during interactions with people who have differing views. In these situations, we may instinctively begin deciding what we are going to say instead of listening. Obstacles can cause missed opportunities during communication.

Completing *Living in Consciousness* will help explore who we are, the reason we are this way and who we want to become. The work will begin by exploring each individual piece of the puzzle that makes up the whole person and how these experiences, beliefs, and ideas speak for and shape us.

Several elements found in *Living in Consciousness*:

- **Activities** will begin with a bit of information and follow up with instructions to work through an exercise.
- **Discussions** provide open question to prompt spontaneous writing. This is an area to explore and express thoughts and memories. There are no right answers, only answers.
- **Scenarios** are provided throughout to serve as examples and thought provoking vignettes.
- **Conscious Reflections** periodically throughout workbook to ponder work completed.

A few tips for completing this workbook:

- Be silent
- Be open-minded
- Be spontaneous
- Be honest with yourself
- Silence your electronics for a few moments
- Do not worry about how your handwriting looks or what words you use.

Enjoy the discovery!

# 1. Workbook

*In order to grow we must look at ourselves in entirety, not just the parts we like.*

## WHO YOU ARE

One of the most important steps to living consciously is to delve into who we are. Similar to putting a puzzle together, we start with unboxing, separating, and making sense of the pieces.

We are each made up of pieces, parts, ideas, beliefs, philosophies, dreams, traditions, emotions, and so much more. We are unique individuals. In order to know or even help others, we must first know ourselves. Many people live their lives on autopilot and rarely ask themselves the questions contained within this workbook. Daily we reinforce who we are, consciously or unconsciously, so there is a bit of a risk in becoming aware of the information. Once you know who you are, the good and the bad, you are faced with a decision; to change the things you wish or accept them as they are, but no longer can you dismiss the existence.

As members of the human race we have many traits in common; yet, each of us has our own unique experiences. For a moment think of the members of a large family. This could be your family or someone else's. Call to mind all of the siblings and their distinctive traits. Each person in the family has his/her own physical characteristics and his/her own outlook and dreams.

On a more universal scale, imagine being in a heavily populated shopping mall when someone runs through the food court and steals an unattended bag sitting on one of the tables. When the police arrive on the scene to take statements and descriptions at least 50 people are able to provide details. When the police compare each statement they have a wide range of differences. The event details and the suspect descriptions varied, even though each person was witness to the same scene.

What is the reason we can see the exact same thing, live in the very same childhood home but have such different takes on things? Each of us brings individual experiences to the present and those experiences are the filter through which we see the world. These differences create interesting dynamics between people. These filters can explain the reason that two people who see the same scene may have polar opposite interpretations. Conflict might arise when the two individuals insist their version is the only option.

This section will explore who you are through open questions for discussions, directed activities, and reflections. Just start writing. Don't overthink what you write. No one has to see your entries. Be as honest as possible to produce the most authentic results

What do you hope to accomplish by working through the workbook of *Living in Consciousness*? _____
_____
_____

What is the best advice you have ever received? _____
_____
_____

What actor/actress would play you in the story of your life? The reason you picked this person? _____
_____
_____

What do you see when you look in the mirror? _____
_____
_____

How do you describe yourself to new people you meet? _____
_____
_____

How would you describe the person you portray at work? _____
_____
_____

How would you describe the person you portray with your friends? _____

_____

_____

How would you describe yourself when you are with your family? _____

_____

_____

How would you describe yourself in romantic relationships? _____

_____

What do you do best? _____

_____

_____

What do you want to improve? _____

_____

_____

Explain the ways you are selfish. _____

_____

_____

Explain the ways you are selfless. _____

_____

_____

What are the payoffs to being selfish/selfless? _____

_____

_____

How does it hurt you to be selfish/selfless? _____

_____

_____

What are your contributions to the world? _____

_____

_____

What do people sometimes pre-judge about you? _____

_____

What motivates you? _____

_____

_____

What do you wish others knew about you? _____

_____

_____

Being satisfied in life is something most people strive toward. What does a satisfying
life look like to you? _____

_____

_____

If you can recall a time in your life you were satisfied, what created that satisfaction. _____

_____

_____

What is your level of commitment to obtaining a satisfying life? _____

_____

_____

## Satisfaction scale

Place yourself on this *satisfaction scale* based on how satisfied you are with your life exactly as it is today.

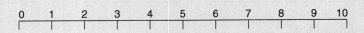

0 is no satisfaction at all

10 is complete satisfaction

# Personality adjectives

When delving into who we are it sometimes helps to have some prompting words. For this activity circle any of the adjectives you believe describe you.

| | | | |
|---|---|---|---|
| Absent-minded | Gentle | Peaceful | Soulful |
| Above average | Guarded | Picky | Soulless |
| Agreeable | Hateful | Plain | Spiteful |
| Ambitious | Helpful | Playful | Stable |
| Apprehensive | Hesitant | Polite | Stern |
| Artistic | Imaginative | Positive | Stoic |
| Assertive | Immature | Powerful | Strong |
| Balanced | Intolerant | Prejudiced | Stupid |
| Brave | Irritable | Proud | Sweet |
| Bright | Joyful | Punctual | Tactful |
| Callous | Judgmental | Quick-tempered | Tactless |
| Careful | Kind | Quiet | Talented |
| Careless | Lame | Realistic | Thoughtful |
| Charming | Lazy | Reassuring | Thoughtless |
| Childish | Level-headed | Reliable | Timid |
| Clever | Loving | Resentful | Tolerant |
| Decisive | Mature | Reserved | Unbalanced |
| Dependent | Mean | Respectful | Uncertain |
| Disruptive | Modest | Restless | Uncooperative |
| Distant | Motivated | Resourceful | Unemotional |
| Eager | Naïve | Sad | Unfriendly |
| Easy-going | Negative | Sassy | Unpopular |
| Egotistical | Nosy | Self-assured | Unsure |
| Emotional | Numb | Sentimental | Vigilant |
| Evasive | Obnoxious | Serious | Warm |
| Experienced | Old-fashioned | Short-tempered | Weak |
| Fabulous | Orderly | Shy | Well-behaved |
| Flabby | Outgoing | Silly | Well-intentioned |
| Frank | Outspoken | Sincere | Well-respected |
| Funny | Passionate | Sloppy | Willing |
| Fussy | Passive | Smart | Worried |
| Generous | Patient | Sophisticated | Zealous |

# BELIEFS AND VALUES

Beliefs and values are an important part of who we are. It is hard to be conscious without knowing what we believe and value. We often acquire our beliefs and values from the people surrounding us during childhood. It helps to explore what we believe and value most before determining how the beliefs and values are working in our life today.

When we live in alignment with our beliefs and values we are more likely to be satisfied. In this section, you will explore what you believe, what you value, and how those beliefs and values are lived.

# The 10 most valuable things

List the 10 most valuable things in your life. Include anything that comes to mind, people, places, things, and events.

| | |
|---|---|
| 1. | 6. |
| 2. | 7. |
| 3. | 8. |
| 4. | 9. |
| 5. | 10. |

# Top five values

Now narrow the list. Use any process of elimination that works best for you to remove 5 from the *10 most valuable things* list. Beside each of your five values, indicate the last time you spent time with that person or engaging in that activity.

| Five Most Valuable | Time Spent |
|---|---|
| 1. | |
| 2. | |

| Five Most Valuable | Time Spent |
|---|---|
| 3. | |
| 4. | |
| 5. | |

*The things we value the most are things we spend time cultivating.*

## Conscious Reflection

*How did it feel to eliminate five things from your list of values?*

*What is the reason you chose the five you kept?*

The beliefs that seem to get us into the most conflict and debate are often the unconscious. A great deal of honesty is necessary to recognize these beliefs. These are the tricky ones because they can interfere on a level that seems we have no control over.

# Unconscious beliefs

Beside each word, jot any thoughts or feelings that come to mind when you read the word. Remember, there is no right or wrong answer. Once you complete the first column use the column to the right to note the reason for your reaction.

| Word | Thoughts or feelings | Reasons |
| --- | --- | --- |
| Police | | |
| Work | | |
| Childhood | | |
| Social Media | | |
| Family | | |
| Education | | |
| Spirituality | | |

What belief(s) do you hold most strongly? _____

_____

_____

What is the reason those beliefs are so important to you? _____

_____

_____

How often do you fight to be right or prove a point? How does that work

out for you? _____

_____

_____

If you engage in debates with others who have different beliefs than you, what do you hope to

accomplish? _____

_____

_____

## Applying beliefs and values

In this section, we will explore the evidence of your beliefs and values by looking at behaviors that do or do not support your claim of these beliefs as if you were stepping into a courtroom to defend, through evidence, these values are important.

How would someone else know the things you value/believe—those on your top five list are important to you? *Example: my children are important to me, so I spend a great deal of quality time with them.*

_____

How do the five things on your list bring you joy? _____

_____

_____

_____

How do the five things on your list bring you stress? _____

_____

_____

_____

How will you contribute more time to the things of value on your list? _____

_____

_____

_____

What beliefs do you hold onto from childhood? _____

_____

_____

_____

# When beliefs and values collide with behavior

There are times when beliefs come into conflict with behavior. Most people will feel guilty when they behave in a way that differs from the way they believe.

Some examples I have heard people give are:

- Overspending when committed to saving money.
- Cheating on a significant other with whom you agreed to monogamy.
- Eating unhealthy while on a diet.

In this section, you will explore what happens to you, internally and externally, when you behave differently than your values.

Feeling guilty for behaving in ways inconsistent with beliefs held strongly isn't negative or unusual. This feeling of guilt motivates us to bring our behavior back in alignment with our beliefs.

Sometimes we can find these beliefs/values are so rigid and ingrained that we are not even conscious about their impact on our decisions. Perhaps, we don't even see them as a choice at all. Take this scenario for example:

# A family holiday

Daisy grew up in a family that celebrated Christmas at her grandmother's home each year. Daisy and all the members of her family had never missed one Christmas. Once she was married and had her own family, she felt guilty for wanting to spend Christmas in her own home. She said:

*I have no choice. I have to go to Grandmother's house.*

When we drilled down into Daisy's beliefs, it appeared she felt obligated to spend Christmas with her grandmother because that is what she had been taught.

*How can you relate to an obligation that feels like you have no choice?*

Consider your strongest beliefs. Discuss what you might feel if your actions were different than your belief. *Example: "I believe making straight As is important. If I made a B I would beat myself up."*

_____

_____

_____

Where do your values and beliefs come into conflict with other people in your life? *Example: I am open-minded and have no problem with interracial dating but my grandmother disagrees. It is hard to be around her when she uses derogatory terms to describe interracial couples.* _____

_____

_____

_____

In your opinion, what makes a behavior or belief right or wrong? _____

_____

_____

_____

How can/do your beliefs help you? _____

_____

_____

How have others pre-judged you in the past? _____

_____

_____

_____

Have you ever heard someone criticize another for not using "common sense"? Consider this for a moment. If we all have different beliefs, values, experiences, and perceptions would it stand to reason that common sense knowledge differs from person to person? This statement is full of judgment, isn't it?

When we believe something we tend to live our life accordingly. How can we prove we believe something, if not by living out that belief? Sometimes when people believe something is wrong they say they *hate it or can't stand it* (like the items you were asked to list earlier in the section). Statements like this limit potential growth and can get in the way of an opportunity to change. This often happens so quickly without our conscious state of mind.

It is uncomfortable at times, but making change requires consciousness. Habits are unconscious and happen as if we are on autopilot. It is as if the unconscious habits force us back into the comfort of what is the norm for our life. This is true even if we don't want to continue down the same path. Change requires acceptance you will be uncomfortable temporarily.

How can/do your beliefs hurt you? _____

_____

_____

What is the advantage of holding onto your beliefs? _____

_____

_____

What is the disadvantage of holding onto your beliefs? _____

_____

_____

_____

What beliefs would you get rid yourself of if you could? _____

_____

_____

_____

What beliefs would you incorporate into your life if you could? _____

_____

_____

_____

What did you learn when you were growing up that you wish you had not learned? _____

_____

_____

_____

How did those things you wish you had not learned when growing up impact you in a negative way? _____

_____

_____

_____

To this point, you may have gained some insights about your thinking process. Recall and reflect on a time you judged someone unfairly before getting to know him or her. _____

_____

_____

_____

_____

_____

_____

_____

_____

*Information is only valuable if you use what you learn.*

## Absolutes

Complete the following statements

I can't stand _____

I hate when _____

I will never _____

I will always _____

These absolute statements are strong. When we begin a statement with "I can't stand," we are suggesting it is impossible to deal with something or someone, but is it really? We may wish things or people were different than they are, but most often we can get through undesirable situations. If we reflect over our life we will probably find many unwanted situations we made it through. We can give ourselves credit. We can handle more than we think. Simply changing the words we use to describe things we do not like can change how we view situations. Give it a try before dismissing the possibility.

## Conscious Reflection

*What are some simple words or phrases you use often that you think are absolutes?*

*Ironically, most of my growth has come through struggle.*

# JUDGMENT AND BIAS

Looking back at the *Unconscious Beliefs* activity, notice how easy it could be for stereotypes and generalizations to become part of a belief system. Most people would not consider themselves judgmental, but everyone has experiences that can unconsciously influence their preconceived notions of others.

In this section, we will explore bias you might hold and judgments you tend to make.

Bias comes from your experience and can unconsciously be picked up from those who surround us in childhood. Each of us is born a blank slate. It is our early environment that writes the script onto that blank slate. Examine these elements in order to identify which beliefs were taught, which are of valuable, which still work, and which are simply repeated due to habit.

We also learn beliefs through experience. For example, if you have been in a series of unhealthy and hurtful relationships you could develop a negative outlook about relationships in general. When we experience an unpleasant situation and replay the events over and over we perpetuate the beliefs we create until they become solidified.

Think of how often you hear yourself or someone else saying things such as:

- All (certain race) are . . .
- All (men/women) are . . .
- All wealthy people . . .

- All people from (certain town) are . . .
- All college students are . . .
- All parents . . .
- All kids . . .
- All drug addicts . . .

These are ingrained generalities from experiences. They are likely unfair oversimplifications, too. These absolute statements can show up in arguments when we have disagreements. Here are a few examples:

- You never . . .
- You always . . .
- Everyone . . .

If we look at the truth against these absolutes, we are likely to see how impossible these statements are to prove. No one always is something or behave in a particular manner. A group of people cannot be sized up to the behavior of one.

## Seeing the world

This activity can produce anxiety for some. It is important to be as honest and open-minded as possible. It can be uncomfortable to talk about prejudices or stereotypes but it is an important conversation to have when fully exploring oneself.

In the first column, I have listed a number of things people can judge. In the two columns to the right, write your reactions, both positive and negative. The final step is to review your positive and negative thoughts again. This time, note in the far right column where you likely learned that thought/belief.

| Potential bias | Positive | Negative | Reasons |
|---|---|---|---|
| The opposite sex | | | |
| Christians | | | |
| Sexual orientation | | | |
| Liberals | | | |
| Police officers | | | |
| Conservatives | | | |
| Rich people | | | |
| Poor people | | | |
| Overweight people | | | |
| College professors | | | |

I want to reiterate that no one's beliefs or opinions are right or wrong. They all serve a purpose. Without taking ownership of our own beliefs, however, they can unconsciously direct us.

This silly exercise can demonstrate how easily we fall into believing something is right or wrong.

## Bath towels

We have all folded—or seen folded—bath towels. Most of us have a particular way to fold them. Answer a few questions to better understand how we can slip into unintended controversy.

1. What are the steps for the way you fold your bath towels?

2. Have you ever had someone help you fold the towels, but they folded them differently?

3. Did you consider the "other" way of folding them the "wrong" way?

4. Where did you learn your towel folding style?

In the grand scheme of life, how important is the way your bath towels are folded?

You may wonder why this matters. Conflicts that spring from right or wrong and good or bad will never be won. Peace will only come to us when we realize each person has had different experiences in life that make each of us unique individuals. Imagine how much time we would lose if we engaged in an argument over how bath towels are "supposed" to be folded. Think of all the other areas where simple conflicts cause breakups, fights, lost jobs, and other conflicts.

# ROLES

Frequently we play roles in life. Maybe you are a mother, a student, an employee, a wife, a daughter, a friend, and the president of the PTO. Those are many roles for one person. There are other roles we can fall into that are not as tangible, but impact us, nonetheless. Examples of these are victim, bully, caretaker, class clown, perfectionist, or tyrant.

Roles are neither good nor bad but can be used to create an identity. If we use our roles to define ourselves, we can forget who we truly are. Behavior is rarely neutral. For each role there is a payoff. Falling into this trap can also be an escape that cuts us off from the truth. When our roles become something we feel we have no control over, we cannot chose otherwise, they can become debilitating.

These roles, even the negative and harmful, have a payoff. All roles have a payoff, even if some excavating is required. Dig a bit into this activity in order to take charge of who you are.

Take a look at these examples people have given me of roles and reasons in their life.

## Victor the victim

During the six months, Victor was in a relationship he had a habit of thinking his girlfriend, Veronica, was mad at him when she didn't text back right away. Victor's self-esteem was low and required frequent confirmation he was cared for. This behavior is a pattern for Victor. He worried he was not good enough, and being in a relationship reassured him, he was valued. Needing this repeated validation was draining.

When Veronica broke up with him, Victor sought comfort from some acquaintances at the local bar. These acquaintances had not seen this behavior from him so said things such as:

*You don't deserve that.*

*You were too good for her anyway.*

*You are a great guy and the right woman is out there for you.*

With this support Victor didn't look at what he might have done to cause problems in this relationship. Instead, he received pats on the back and reinforcements of the belief that he was the victim.

**PAYOFF:** In relationships both parties contribute to the enrichment or destruction. Victor has things he could change to contribute to the health of a future relationship, if he would remove himself from the role of victim.

# Betty the boss

Betty was the CEO of the crisis center in her small community. She worked an average of 80 hours each week and often brought work home. She was often seen taking phone calls at all hours and walking out of the room to handle a crisis calls. Betty took those calls, responded to texts and e-mail despite what she was doing elsewhere, including her son's soccer games, family dinners, holidays, weekends, on vacations, and even at a recent dance recital her daughter was performing. Her husband noticed Betty working more when there was more discord within their family.

This crisis center was crucial to the welfare of many in this small town. Betty was something of a hero to her neighbors. She received much recognition and won various awards throughout the years. As she ran out of the dance recital, for instance, a few people turned to one another complimenting her for the sacrifice she made for the community. Betty also received kudos when she returned and heard comments such as:

*I don't know how you do everything you do, you are an angel!*
*Where do you get the energy to be Superwoman?*

**PAYOFF:** Betty was given frequent praise and rewarded for her role even though it was at the expense of her own time and family. It also seemed that she was able to avoid any conflict happening with her own family while keeping herself busy with the crises of others.

# Patti the people pleaser

Patti was a recent college graduate. She graduated in half the time as her peers and was recognized with honors. Patti had been a straight A Grade student since elementary school and was met with high expectations throughout her life. Patti received frequent accolades for her academic achievements and felt pressure to succeed.

Patti received rewards and recognition but her mother did not give her approval if she was not excelling. She even pursued a degree in an area where the pay was high but she had little interest, because her mother insisted. Patti was offered an unpaid internship in China, but her mother refused to talk to her for several days after hearing the news.

**PAYOFF:** Though she longed to go to China she was willing to compromise her happiness for her mother's approval.

Consider how your responses might be different than Victor, Betty, and Patti?

In this section, you can explore roles that you may use to represent yourself and the payoff.

## Reasons for roles

| Role | How it looks | Payoff |
|------|--------------|--------|
|      |              |        |
|      |              |        |
|      |              |        |
|      |              |        |
|      |              |        |
|      |              |        |

*As long as I can blame someone else for my problems, I do not have to change.*

## Roleplaying

In the first column place the roles you play.

In the second column indicate how that role possibly looks to observers on the outside.

In the final column note the payoff for each image.

| Role | From the outside | The reason/payoff |
|------|------------------|-------------------|
| Example: Perfectionist | Cold hearted and uncaring, standoffish, distant, flawless | If I stay away from people they cannot hurt me |
|      |                  |                   |
|      |                  |                   |

| Role | From the outside | The reason/payoff |
|------|------------------|-------------------|
|  |  |  |
|  |  |  |
|  |  |  |
|  |  |  |

## Conscious Reflection

*How did it feel to complete this activity?*

*Discuss the roles you would like to stop playing and the reasons.*

# Limitations of labeling

To this point we have explored our unique personalities, roles, beliefs—conscious and unconscious—values and even bias. We likely agree that each of us come from somewhere; have specific traits, stories, and experiences. Understanding these distinctions for our own growth is important and appreciating them in others is effective for communication. Often people with diagnoses feel bound to being labeled instead of a being referred to as a person.

Though each of us has roles, it is crucial not to fall into the trap of labeling others. People are much more complex than one role, one belief, or one event. For the ultimate encounter with another human being it is important to remember we do not know the entirety of their journey or experience until we allow them to tell their stories.

A positive outcome of taking on this challenge to know oneself better will open an opportunity to understand others. Once we cease an outward expression of judgment or labeling, we can journey inward and begin seeking more understanding of human intricacies. The genuine appreciation for and desire to know another from their perspective instead of our pre-conceived idea of them will allow us to see them authentically.

## Person first language

One place we create our own obstacles in communication and connection is through simple sentence structure. When we refer to others with labels we diminish their wholeness. Eliminating this derogatory barrier becomes effortless when we make a habit of referring to the person before a label. Here are a few examples:

| Previous reference | | Simple change |
|---|---|---|
| Jim is a recovering alcoholic | ➠ | Jim is a person in recovery |
| Mary is autistic | ➠ | Mary is a person with autism |
| Andrea is handicapped | ➠ | Andrea is a person with a physical disability |
| Samuel is mentally ill | ➠ | Samuel is a person who has mental illness |

This applies to areas other than diagnoses. When referring to a person's race, religion, sexual orientation, etc. refer to anyone as a person, most importantly. As minor as this seems, a simple shift in language will show respect instead of judgment.

## PERCEPTION

The best way to view perception is, simply, how we see the world and the contents. Each of us has unique perceptions. Our perceptions are like our own pair of lenses through which we see the world. Knowing each of us has our own perceptions helps us realize the importance of understanding someone instead of judging them.

In this section, you will come away with a better understanding of how you are perceived, how you perceive others, and the reason for these perceptions.

From previous sections of *Living in Consciousness,* we already know our judgments are based on *our* beliefs and values, and not those of the other person. When we do this we are making up our own stories about what the other person meant, felt, and believes. Doing this will cause disagreements.

Pessimistic people create perceptions for themselves that can cause undue drama and strife. Instead of changing to a more positive perspective, a pessimistic person might live in lifelong discontent believing they have no choice in the matter.

The story below is an example of how perception can cause a person to create a story that stirs up his or her own frustration.

# A grocery store incident

Sam was in the checkout line at the local grocery store last week. A person stepped in front of him in line. Sam became angry and made up this story about what the person who stepped in front of him intended:

Sam: This lady has no respect for anyone else. She didn't even look at me. She is so selfish and rude and thinks she can do anything she wants no matter whom else is in the way.

Stepping in front of another person in a checkout line without acknowledging them may be rude, no doubt, but does Sam really know the story he made up to be factual? He does not. He is simply seeing the situation through *his* lenses and deciding her intentions based on what he would do in a similar situation. This is a simple example of daily events that often cause us conflict, stress, frustration, and a number of negative feelings and possible behaviors. Because we would not behave in a particular manner does not mean everyone is the same. When we hold others up to our own measuring stick we will often be disappointed.

Making up stories about another person's intentions only creates stress for you.

How do you perceive yourself? _____

_____

_____

What do you like about yourself? _____

_____

_____

What do you dislike about yourself? _____

_____

_____

What things do you "beat yourself up" over? _____

_____

_____

What things do you do that you are proud of? _____

_____

_____

What do you wish you did better? _____

_____

_____

When someone close to you gives you feedback about changes you could make, how do you respond?

_____

_____

_____

*Without examining patterns in our life we are likely to continue on the same path.*

# How others perceive you

The way others perceive us is as important as the way we perceive others. Once we become aware of how we are perceived we can remain conscious of our impact on others.

In this section, we will explore how others perceive you. Let's start right off with an activity.

Take a look at the three possibilities to decide how you most often react to how you are perceived by others.

- Overly concerned with the way others perceive me. I am troubled when I make someone unhappy and go out of my way to fix it or I think about it over and over wishing I could change how the person feels.

- I do not care how others perceive me. I am who I am and make no apologies.

- I am true to myself but am open to receiving feedback from others.

You may have already guessed that the last example is the healthiest of the three provided. It is as important to know who you are, what you believe and stand for, as it is to be aware of the impact you have on others. Speaking your mind is not without consequences if you are injurious to others in that process.

Discuss how four or five people in your life would describe you by completing the following exercise. Feel free to pick any of the important people in your life.

*Person 1*:_____

How would this person describe you? _____

_____

_____

What are the reasons you believe this person might have this/these perception(s)? _____

_____

_____

How do you agree with this description? _____

_____

_____

How would you disagree with this description? _____

_____

_____

How is your perception of this person impacted by their opinion of you? _____
_____
_____

*Person 2*: _____

How would this person describe you? _____
_____
_____

What are the reasons you believe this person might have this/these perception(s)? _____
_____
_____

How do you agree with this description? _____
_____
_____

How would you disagree with this description? _____
_____
_____

How is your perception of this person impacted by their opinion of you? _____
_____
_____

*Person 3*: _____

How would this person describe you? _____
_____
_____

What are the reasons you believe this person might have this/these perception(s)? _____
_____
_____

How do you agree with this description? _____
_____
_____

How would you disagree with this description? _____

_____

_____

How is your perception of this person impacted by their opinion of you? _____

_____

_____

*Person 4*: _____

How would this person describe you? _____

_____

_____

What are the reasons you believe this person might have this/these perception(s)? _____

_____

_____

How do you agree with this description? _____

_____

_____

How would you disagree with this description? _____

_____

_____

How is your perception of this person impacted by their opinion of you? _____

_____

_____

*Person 5*: _____

How would this person describe you? _____

_____

_____

What are the reasons you believe this person might have this/these perception(s)? _____

_____

_____

How do you agree with this description? _____

_____

_____

How would you disagree with this description? _____

_____

_____

How is your perception of this person impacted by their opinion of you? _____

_____

_____

# Differences between perceptions

In this section, we will explore difference between how you see yourself and how others see you.

What are the differences between the way you perceive yourself and the way others perceive you?_____

_____

_____

_____

How do you respond when someone in your life asks you to change behaviors they do not like? _____

_____

_____

How do you respond when someone in your life asks you to change the behaviors they believe have a negative impact?

_____

_____

How do you handle situations when someone in your life is behaving in a way you do not like? _____

_____

_____

_____

After taking a look at your perceptions and those of others it is helpful to determine patterns of conflict between the two. Only we can change our behavior to assist us in enriching our relationships. Even when we view ourselves as the victim and another person as being at fault we must take ownership of our own happiness and behavior.

# Conflicts

In the first column recall people with whom you had conflict in the past.

In the middle column note the reason(s) for the conflict.

In the remaining column discuss the most often outcome of the conflicts.

| Person | Reason | Outcome |
|---|---|---|
| *Example:* *Barbara* | *She wouldn't take out the trash* | *I would yell and slam the doors. She would sulk and not talk to me for three days.* |
|  |  |  |
|  |  |  |
|  |  |  |
|  |  |  |
|  |  |  |
|  |  |  |

Two healthy individuals have trust in one another, share differing views, and offer one another feedback when necessary.

**Conflict** is not an unusual or negative trait of healthy interactions. Resolving conflict is not always comfortable, but is growth producing and turns out to be an enriching interaction between people who have strong self-worth and a clear awareness of self.

Sometimes the beliefs held unconsciously can trigger a conflict. When someone does not live up to the expectation you have on them it can cause problems. This *isn't right or wrong*. It may simply be a matter of different beliefs or expectations. It is important to acknowledge differences and allow all parties the respect of their opinions.

If we want to stop having conflicts, we have to determine the root cause of them. Recall the bath towel scenario. If someone were to have an argument about how the towels should be folded, it is likely the real reason for the argument is much deeper than bath towels and is connected to an historic event.

What changes could you possibly make in your life in order to have fewer conflicts with those people you discussed in the activity? Remember to only focus on you, not changes you would want the other person to make.

What patterns do you see with the type of conflicts that occurred? _____

_____

_____

What patterns do you see with the outcomes? _____

_____

_____

What patterns do you see with your behaviors? _____

_____

_____

*When delving into your history*
*it is vital to identify patterns.*

***Conflict*** *is a normal trait*
*in healthy interaction.*

## Conflict triggers

Conflict happens for a reason and the topic of the conflict is often only a symptom of an underlying cause. It is likely the conflict will continue if we do not identify and resolve the actual cause.

In the first column transfer the people from the Conflicts activity.

In the center column note the wish or want you had in each circumstance.

In the last column identify the cause (trigger) of the conflict.

| Person | Wish/Want | Actual cause (trigger) |
|---|---|---|
| *Example:* *Barbara* | *I wish she would take out the trash when I am at work* | *When she doesn't take out the trash it feels like me working all day isn't noticed or she doesn't care how hard I work* |
| | | |
| | | |
| | | |
| | | |
| | | |
| | | |

# THE IMPACT OF HISTORY

Many times the real reason for current conflict is related to events from the past. Unconscious emotions can be similar to a buoy on a lake. Beneath the water lies an anchor that sits at the bottom of the lake.

The buoy represents the current conflict and the anchor symbolizes the historic event. This is not abnormal but causes unnecessary harm to our current relationships. Knowing our history and where it shows up in harmful ways in our present life is vital. When we are aware we can avoid our history from negatively impacting the present.

# Your triggers

Delve into what events *from the past* might have been the root cause of this reaction.

| Person | What it triggers inside | Historic event |
|---|---|---|
| *Example:* *Barbara* | When she doesn't take out the trash it feels like me working all day isn't noticed or she doesn't care how hard I work | When I was growing up my mom never told me I was doing a good job no matter how hard I worked |
| | | |
| | | |
| | | |
| | | |

# Feedback

Hearing how we come across to others is not easy for everyone. If we do not hear those who surround us when they provide this valuable information we miss an opportunity to grow for the better. Some people treat strangers better than those whom they have a relationship.

# Angelica's anger

When Angelica talks to others she is extremely loud and she rejects what others are saying by putting her hand up to interrupt them when they speak. Others attempt to offer her their thoughts on how she comes across to them.

Angelica dismisses them by saying:

> *Whatever. I have always been this way. That is just your opinion. I don't care.*

# Tom's temper

When Tom is given advice on how to behave he follows the advice. This has happened repeatedly when given suggestions by anyone, co-workers, family, friends, and a few times even strangers online.

Tom says:

> *I care what others think. I like when people around me are happy. I accept all advice.*

A balance between the two is most helpful to our own growth, as well as those we care for.

# Balanced Becky

Becky cares about others and her impact. She also knows who she is and wants to be. Her boundaries are healthy and she stays aware of her behaviors and their impact on others. After a recent employee meeting a co-worker told Becky, she was offended about being interrupted during the meeting and not allowed to contribute to the discussion the way she wanted.

Beck said to her:

*Thank you for telling me this. I will be more aware of everyone wanting to contribute in the future. Would you like to spend some time to share your thoughts with me now?*

Receiving feedback is not always easy but would you rather live the rest of your life driving people away? When we care for others it is important we appropriately enhance those relationships by continuing to remain open. Being open is equally important to giving and receiving feedback when warranted. In my opinion, those who love and support us have permission to hold a mirror up to us when it is for our benefit. It is crucial to understand this does not work well in relationships where there is not first trust, safety, and security.

If we are not in the habit of giving or receiving feedback it is important to practice. Like any behavior that comes naturally it is first learned. Though I often hear people ask why they should be the one to initiate this level of communication when the other person has not tried to do so. My answer is simple. Someone has to start. If not you, then who will take the first step? If not now, then when will it happen? Relationships are enriched when people work through tough times. They are broken down when tough times are not discussed but only swept under the rug.

People are not perfect, including each of us. We cannot continue to make excuses for the damage of our interactions with others. If we want a different outcome we have to try something new. Blaming the other person (significant other, co-workers, parents, professors, clients) is a convenient excuse for not changing yourself. Consider following these steps.

## WIT

**W**hat:
What do you want to convey? What do you hope the person hears? Think through the words you will use. Prepare to use language that does not place blame or increase the defensiveness for either party.

**I**ntention:
What is the reason you want to share this? What are you hoping to get out of telling the person this information? Do not provide feedback in an attempt to harm the other person. This further damages the relationship. Do not fight simply to prove yourself right. There is no winner in this conversation and it will likely cause harm.

**T**iming:
Consider the best time to have a conversation. Do not talk about important issues when your emotions are running high. Do not attempt to have important conversations when either person only has a few minutes. Have this conversation when both of you can sit down and talk. Also ask the other person if they are open to the conversation before you begin.

> *Communication is necessary to living a healthy life. You can't sweep something broken into a bag and call it whole. It takes repair.*

# CHOICE

*I have to. I have no choice.*

You have heard people use that expression before. Perhaps, you have used those words. What causes people to believe they have no choice?

Before we go further into the roots of beliefs and behaviors it is important that we discuss choice and responsibility. Those who surround us mold us during childhood. Some children have positive and nurturing environments. Others have rigid environments. Still other's environments are harmful. Even if our childhood influences are unhealthy or had a negative impact, once we are adults we are the only responsible party for the remainder of life. Continuing to be unhappy, unhealthy, and placing blame toward the past keeps us stuck.

Blaming people in our life today is futile. Each situation we find unfulfilling cannot be changed by others. We are each responsible for our own happiness. If we blame others but long to be happy, there is a choice to make.

## Store clerk

Charles works in the local drugstore as a checkout clerk. He does not like his job but says:

> *I have no choice. I have to work. I have bills to pay.*

When Charles has customers his negative non-verbal communication is excessive. It is not difficult to know how Charles feels about his job. Here are some of the behaviors:

- Loud sighs.
- Lack of eye contact.
- Robotic comments, such as "Welcome to the store." "Is this all?" without emotion.
- Typing hard onto the register keys.
- Lack of sincerity.

The last day Charles worked, a customer attempted to make conversation with him. When he robotically said to a customer walking through the entrance, "*Welcome to the store.*" His register customer joked, "*I bet you say that in your sleep since you say it all day long.*" A sarcastic Charles replied back, "*That is just part of the soul stealing process of this job I have to do. I have no choice.*"

Charles is obviously unhappy and believes he has no other choice.

What causes a person to stay where they are unhappy, to be bound by things they detest? You could be a person like this yourself. If you are not you probably know someone who is perpetually unhappy, discontent, broken, disappointed, dismissive, negative, passive aggressive, and sarcastic? We have all been broken. What is the reason some will not let go of the bitterness? Do they know the amount of energy—and life—it requires? I propose this is a choice.

What is the payoff? When a person says they want to be happy but do not seek peace they are getting a payoff from that decision. Perhaps, a person who can throw up their hands and claim they have no choice or clench their fist and blame another for the results in their life are allowing themselves to take no responsibility for their own life. Allowing another person or situation to dictate how one will feel and respond on a daily basis allows this person to remain stuck. They are not necessarily doing this on purpose. Without soul searching, similar to the awareness *Living in Consciousness* can bring, one can remain unconsciousness of the cause and one's own ability to change his/her perspective.

Life is not always the way we want. Our first responsibility is to be honest about what we want. If the situation will not change, we have a few options. We can: Accept things as they are, change our perspective, or leave the situation.

There are no other alternatives but in those three options there is great freedom. If we decide to stay in a place or with people we do not prefer, we are making a choice to accept the place or people. Unless you make the choice to be content with and work out what life provides, you will choose to live in a state of terminal awfulness. A shift in perspective can assist being more content with your life.

Consider what situations or person(s) you allow to control your happiness, what you get out of staying stuck, and how you might feel if you were able to release the control your history has on today.

## Resolution

| Person or situation | Payoff | Relieved with resolution |
|---|---|---|
|  |  |  |
|  |  |  |
|  |  |  |
|  |  |  |
|  |  |  |
|  |  |  |

## Have to

List everything you believe you *have to do* on a daily, weekly, or monthly basis.

Look over your list again and make sure these are things you **have to** do.

Mark through any items on your list that have an alternative like the example below then use the following activity to decide the alternatives.

| Pay rent | Work | Exercise | Go to school |
|---|---|---|---|

*If there is an alternative you are not being forced, you are making a choice.*

| "Have to" item marked through above | Alternative |
|---|---|
| Exercise | I could be out of shape instead |
| | |
| | |
| | |
| | |

When there is an alternative to the item on your list it is not something you "have to" do. Instead, it is a choice. It may not be your preference but it is not something you are being forced to do. The more we can eliminate words like "have to" from our vocabulary the more free we will feel and the more responsibility we will have over our own lives. When your alarm rings in the morning consider getting up as a choice. This could change your outlook on the day. Changing your outlook can change the outcome.

# PIECES OF THE PUZZLE

We have established that everyone came from somewhere and have a story to tell. Our histories are pieces woven into the complete puzzle of who we are.

In this section, we will help pull apart the major pieces that make up the full picture. These parts do not have to be labeled as good or bad. Often it can be emotional to look back at the details, but taking it apart for examination to look at each piece separately can protect from the depth of emotions.

Understanding this history can help us understand who we are today. Each thing we experience/learn in our early years becomes part of what guides our life. From birth until an adult we are inundated with influence from others. Some of the most lasting impressions are made before 10 years old.

To complete this section of the workbook, you might consider reaching out to your family members for some of the answers. Many times there are events that a family will not talk about because of how uncomfortable the topic.

Physical traits are genetic, like eye color, height, shoe size, and predisposition to disease. These cannot be changed, only be monitored. For instance, if your family has a history of heart disease, you cannot change the fact that it is part of your genetic makeup. However, using this information you can make changes in your behavior (such as eating better), which may help decrease your risk of heart disease.

Just as your physical DNA impacts the person you are, so does the environment. You learn your role and expected behavior from the people who surround you in your childhood. It is likely that many of the people surrounding you did not even realize this was programming you.

Families do not usually have a "sit down" meeting with the kids to let them know the programming plans. I do not believe parents make a plan to carry out intentional harms toward their children. I cannot envision parents sitting down together saying, "Let's mess this kid up!" Most people parent the way they were parented, healthy or unhealthy. Each of these pieces fit together to make a whole life experience. Unlike physical DNA, environmental DNA does not have to be permanent. It will take time, hard work, soul searching, and consciousness but environmental DNA can be changed.

There are many pieces to who we are. They tell our story. All the pieces work together to make a whole person. One of the pieces may have a more profound impact than another but each is woven together to create a unique individual. One or two events in a whole life do not define an individual.

The pieces are where, when, spirituality, financial, media, education, employment, social, rules, culture, and who surrounded us.

## Physical

Simply put an **X** in the columns that correspond with the condition and person genetically linked to that condition.

| Condition | Self | Father | Mother | Paternal Grandparent(s) | Maternal Grandparent(s) |
|---|---|---|---|---|---|
| Heart Disease | | | | | |
| Diabetes | | | | | |
| High Blood Pressure | | | | | |
| Cystic Fibrosis | | | | | |
| Huntington's | | | | | |
| Arthritis | | | | | |
| Blood Clots | | | | | |
| Cancer | | | | | |
| Asthma | | | | | |
| Depression | | | | | |
| ADHD | | | | | |
| High Cholesterol | | | | | |
| Stroke | | | | | |
| Sickle Cell Anemia | | | | | |
| Celiac Disease | | | | | |
| Addiction | | | | | |
| Mental Health Concerns | | | | | |
| Other | | | | | |

What impact does your physical DNA have on your life? _____

_____

_____

Discuss how the members in your family affected by any of the conditions on the chart handled or avoided taking care of the condition(s). _____

_____

_____

What precautions/actions might you take in your life in order to avoid falling victim to some of the medical conditions woven into your physical DNA? _____

_____

_____

Have you been diagnosed with any medical conditions? _____

_____

_____

How open are family members about any health concerns they have experienced in their life? _____

_____

_____

Mental health and addiction diagnoses are brain disorders but are stigmatized by society as being moral deficiencies. While you cannot know their inner thoughts, what are your speculations on what your family thought/thinks of people who have mental health or addiction concerns? _____

_____

_____

How are your views similar or different than your family about mental health and addiction? _____

_____

*We consider our physical DNA while ignoring the possibility we have DNA from our environment, too. The people we grow up with greatly influence the person we become. Thank goodness those DNA strands can be unwound. Unwound with a lot of introspection, honesty, desire, and consciousness*

# Environmental

***Where***: This is the actual place you grew up, including the physical dwelling and community in which you lived. Where we grow up impacts us. For instance, living in a rural versus urban area is vastly different. Neither is better or worse but each of these provides different experiences. Some things you might consider are the state(s), region(s), neighborhood(s), and part(s) of the world you lived. Also, the habits, traditions, or conventions that were part of the culture that build part of this structure. The size of the school you attended contributes to where you were raised, as well as the type of school you attend (public versus private, for example).

If you lived in multiple places as a child refer to any of the places you would like.

Describe the place(s) you refer to as home. _____

_____

_____

How have the place(s) you were raised impacted the person you have become? _____

_____

_____

Describe the neighborhood(s) where you grew up. _____

_____

_____

What are some things you liked about the place(s) you grew up? _____

_____

_____

What are some of the things you disliked about the place(s) you grew up? _____

_____

_____

Describe the community/communities that surrounded you while you were growing up. _____

_____

_____

Where did you feel most safe as you grew up? _____

_____

_____

What might you change about the place(s) you grew up, if you were able? _____

_____

_____

_____

**When**: This piece of the puzzle is the time period, which we were born. The generation we are born into creates a distinction between others and us. *When we* can also include the decade, the generation or era. The time frame we were born had social issues that impacted our life experiences. These issues ultimately color the eyes with which we see the world.

Contrasts between generations create challenges when each person does not take time to understand the other. Many people believe generational stereotypes. As we have discussed previously in this workbook, what we know is what we do. Often, as children our elders expected us to behave in the same way they would have in similar circumstances. As adults we likely understand that our elders only wanted what was best for us when they began lectures with, "back when I was your age . . ." Unfortunately, children do not have the capacity for understanding intention.

Imagine the differences between someone who was born in a generation without indoor plumbing or telephones versus those born into a world where smart phones were the norm.

An element of improved communication includes being familiar with other generations, as well. When we better understand others and ourselves it this further heightens our exchanges.

- The traditional Generation (1900–1945)
- Baby Boomer Generation (1946–1964)
- Generation X (1965–1980)
- **Millennials (1981–2000)**

When were you born? _____

How does the generation you were raised in, influence the person you are today? _____

_____

_____

What are your fondest memories about growing up in your generation? _____

_____

_____

_____

If you could pick another generation to have grown up, which would it be and what is the reason? _____

_____

_____

Discuss any conflicts you had as a result of generation gaps/differences during childhood.

_____

_____

_____

What were the conflicts? _____

_____

_____

What was different about their generation than the one you were raised? _____

_____

_____

What must it have been like to be raised during your parent's generation? _____

_____

_____

*Spirituality*: Often spirituality is confused with religion. While religion can make up your spirituality, it is not necessary. When discussing spirituality, I am essentially referring to our purpose. The reason you were put on earth. Questions to consider while exploring the influence of spirituality on you could be: How did your family feel about a purpose, drive, or vision? How was religion viewed? How were questions about spirituality fielded and answered? Were you able to have views different from those practiced in your childhood?

Discuss the spirituality practiced in your childhood. _____

_____

_____

Discuss how the spirituality practiced in the home you were raised impacted the person you have become. _____

_____

_____

How free were you to explore your purpose in the home you grew up? _____

_____

_____

How different are your views today than those practiced in your childhood home? _____

_____

_____

What is your purpose? _____

_____

_____

_____

*Leave people better than you found them.*

**Financial**: It is important to understand this does not automatically mean money. Instead, take a look at how money was treated, valued, and handled by those significant to you during your childhood. Consider how driven they were to obtain money and how they took care of the money they attained. Think of what you were and were not taught about money management. Also think through the impact finances had on your life, the socio-economic class of your household, if paying bills was important, difficult, or discussed. Were you given things in place of time and attention? Did anyone talk about money fixing problems? Were finances sufficient to provide basic needs?

Discuss the type of financial environment in your childhood family. _____

_____

_____

_____

Discuss how your childhood impacted the person you have become in relation to finances.

_____

_____

_____

What kind of security did you have with finances? Consider if money was feared, sought after, or simply something to provide for your needs. Also discuss how this impacted the way you handle and view finances today. _____

_____

_____

How charitable was the family in which you grew up? _____

_____

_____

How is your management and views on finances different and the same as what you learned growing up? _____

_____

_____

*Media* has long had an influence on us. Television commercials tell us how to fix any ailment we have. Sitcoms convey earth-shaking events, fix them, and live happily ever after within 30 minutes. The news shows give us glimpses into tragic issues multiple times per day. The more advanced technology becomes the more inundated we are with thoughts, opinions, and tragedy. Consider the impact from media on your childhood. How much time did you invest in television, radio, technology? Were you born before all homes had personal computers or in a time when everyone had smart phones? What we take in gets into our unconscious.

Texting and e-mail, instead of a phone call have become the norm. Nonverbal communication (e-mail and texting) does not provide each participant the emotional fulfillment that usually occurs during verbal interactions. When having a verbal conversation we communicate more than just the words we are speaking, to include tone, volume, and emotions through laughter, crying, sighing, and yawning. If a friend were to call you today and they were very excited or crying, would your emotions not change accordingly? Does seeing LOL in a text make you laugh the same as you might if you heard the same message with the other person laughing?

Social media has added another component of influence today. Social media often does not portray the whole person hidden behind the keyboard. If we compare our lives with those we see depicted on social media, we will likely feel we do not measure up.

How much time do you currently spend in the presence of television, radio, other technology, and social media?

_____

_____

How much media input do you use to inform you? _____

_____

_____

What is your payoff of engaging in social media? _____

_____

_____

> *Social media allows the individual to portray their ideal self while controlling the amount of their emotional commitment; which is not always possible during face-to-face interactions.*

*Education*: Consider the level of education of those in your home, the importance placed on education, and the expectations for your education. Think back, to how free were you to decide if you might attend college or what major you decided to pursue. In this area, it helps to look at how attendance, punctuality, and homework were seen by your elders during your childhood education. Consider the elementary, middle, and high school(s) you attended and their environment. Reflect on your teachers, subjects, and extracurricular activities.

I once worked with Molly, a client, who was the first person in her family to graduate high school. Her high school counselor helped her apply for several colleges and scholarships. She received an academic scholarship to complete an Associates degree at a local community college. I was so excited for her.

Paula: Your parents must be so proud.

Molly: No they aren't.

Paula: What is the reason they are not?

Molly: Everyone in my family thinks I am trying to act better than them. My sister even said, "Oh, you think you are better than me?"

I learned a lot from that conversation. Sometimes families do not want us to accomplish more or be different from them. I do not believe this is about the desire to hurt us. I propose this is about being uncomfortable or even fearful. Like the human body, our families attempt to maintain homeostasis, even when "normal" is dysfunctional or maladaptive.

How would you describe the type of student you were in childhood? _____

_____

_____

How were your relationships with teachers or other school personnel? _____

_____

_____

How did your popularity influence your enjoyment of school? _____

_____

_____

Discuss the importance of education in the household you were raised. _____

_____

_____

Discuss how the view of education by those you were raised around, had on the person you have become. _____

_____

How much of an influence do the people you were raised by and around, still have on the direction and selection of your educational path? _____

_____

What impact did the schools you attended have on your attitude and perspective toward education?_____

_____

_____

_____

What happened in your household and at school if you failed a class? _____

_____

_____

_____

What happened in your household and at school if you excelled? _____

_____

_____

_____

How would your family react if you decided to pursue a different educational path? _____

_____

_____

_____

How are your educational goals different/similar to those of your family members? _____

_____

_____

# Crabs

When sharing good news about success with people she has known all of her life, Molly was met with disapproval. Did her family want her to fail? Did they want her to stay stuck? They would likely tell you no. So, what is the reason they were not enthusiastic about her opportunity to surpass their success? Maybe fear? This story reminds me of another I have used many times about unhealthy families or communities who don't rally around another person's success.

When crabbing near the ocean, I noticed there was no need to put a cover on the cooler we used to contain the crabs. When any of the crabs attempted to crawl out of the cooler, the others would pull them back down.

Any disruption to status quo is uncomfortable to the entire system. When we want to do something that is never done before it causes a great deal of fear and discomfort. In order to break free from this, we have to be aware of that possibility. If we give into the fear of the family, we will not be able to live out our purpose.

***Employment***: Contemplate how your adult role models viewed employment. Think back to what they communicated about the value of a job and the loyalty they showed to their employer. Consider how often they worked as opposed to how often they were out of work. Reflect on their attendance and punctuality at work. Speculate the value they placed on being employed.

Whether or not they directly communicated with you about their employment, it is likely you understood their attitude toward employment.

What kind of work did those in your childhood do? _____

_____

_____

How similar or different a career path have you chosen? _____

_____

_____

Discuss the importance of employment within the environment you were raised. _____

_____

_____

Discuss what impact the view of employment, by those you were raised around, had on the person you have become. _____

_____

_____

How much of an influence do the people you were raised by and around, still have on the direction of your career and attitude toward your job? _____

_____

_____

How supported are you about your career choice? _____

_____

_____

*Social*: This area includes friends, peers, social events attended, and leisure activities engaged in by people in your childhood home. Think back about the friends, the people in your home kept, and the view they had of friends you chose. How welcome were others into your household? Look at the household's involvement in, and types of, social activities in which members participated. What were your hobbies? Did your family enjoy your hobbies, as well? Were social engagements a family or individual event? What did your family do for fun?

Discuss the importance of friends in the environment you were raised. _____

_____

_____

What did your family do for fun? _____

_____

Share about any friends you had that were unwelcome in your home or you might have been discouraged from keeping. _____

_____

_____

What types of friends and friendships did your parents have? _____

_____

_____

What do you wish were different about the social activities when you were growing up? _____

_____

Discuss your best childhood friend. _____

_____

_____

Share some memories of social activities with people in your childhood. _____

_____

_____

***Rules***: We learn about authority early in our lives. How simple rules are established, enforced, and the consequences given are vital. These impact how we view rules, policies, laws, and authority the remainder of our life. When exploring this puzzle piece, think back to how law enforcement, employers, teachers, coaches, and elders were viewed in your younger years. Also consider how consistent, rigid or relaxed rules in your home were. Were you given latitude to break a rule and learn a lesson or were you ruled under an iron fist and not allowed to explore boundaries?

Discuss the importance of rules in the environment you were raised. _____

_____

_____

What are some of the rules you recall from your childhood environment? _____

_____

_____

What would happen when you broke rules? _____

_____

_____

Did you strictly adhere to those rules or did you rebel? How was that rewarded/punished in your home? _____

_____

_____

What was punishment like for you in childhood? _____

_____

_____

More important than how these rules were enforced is how you have carried this into your adult life. Sometimes when one is governed with rigid restrictions they become rigid themselves or they rebel against this. When rules are inconsistent—one day something is vitally important and the next it is forgotten—children often question their boundaries.

Discuss how the view of rules by those you were raised around had on the person you have become. _____

_____

*Culture:* Our culture bonds us with a group of people that include values, beliefs, traditions, language, patterns, skills, knowledge, and even objects. Our culture is communicated through experience. These are "just things we do" because we are involved in this way of life from birth. Our culture can bring a sense of meaning because we belong to a larger group of people than only those who live in our household. Members of the same culture often act, think, and believe in a manner, which is similar to the rest of the group. Our race, heritage, and ethnicity can also be part of this piece of the puzzle.

Looking into your culture can connect many pieces of the puzzle to create a clearer picture of you.

Our culture, like all of the other puzzle pieces, is normal for us. We rarely know any other way of life when we are growing up. We usually do not see other ways of life until we are older. By then, we may be interested in exploring other cultures or think other cultures are odd. Other cultures are not odd but simply different than our own. I encourage you to explore other cultures to see their intricacies.

With which culture do you most identify? _____

Culture is made up of many things. Think of how each of these showed up in your childhood uniquely: Symbols, values, language, faith, stories, and food. Sometimes they may be harder to identify in our own culture because they become a common part of our lives. Identifying these in other cultures you can see how they standout.

## Culture pie

*Who*: The people who made up our childhood are the strongest influences we had. To a certain age we likely had little contact with people outside of the home. The traditions, attitudes, behaviors, and relationship with the people closest to us during our younger years become the norm and the ruler by which we measure everything else throughout our lifetime.

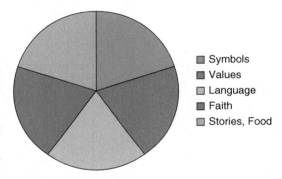

■ Symbols
■ Values
■ Language
■ Faith
■ Stories, Food

It is important to drill down into our early years by considering each person who had an impact from birth until teenage years. Sometimes people feel guilty when completing this because they see it as passing judgment of people they are loyal to. This is not about passing judgment; instead it is a fact-finding mission. Without looking deeper into the people who surrounded our early years it will be hard to review the patterns.

We learn from our parents, other adults, and siblings in our childhood home simply by being present. Whether healthy or dysfunctional, we learn:

| How to | | |
|---|---|---|
| Parent | Drive | Cook |
| Clean | Resolve conflict | Handle stress |
| Nurture | Treat people | Communicate |
| **How to be** | | |
| A friend | A family member | A customer |
| A neighbor | A child to an adult parent | A member of society |
| An employee | A spouse | Punctual |

The adults in our childhood never have to sit us down and tell us they are going to teach us these lessons, we simply learn by what we see, hear, and miss out on. Think about the example given earlier about folding bath towels. If we learn something as simple as that in our childhood, imagine how many other daily intricacies we learn.

Children are even taught by things they do not see or hear. When adults keep secrets from children and believe the child does not know something is going on, they are mistaken. Children can often feel tension in a home even when there are no words spoken.

When parents are absent they teach their children something. Absent parents impact their children through the void left by their absence.

Finally, divorced parents who use their children to hurt the other person damage those children mightily.

Children learn from everything they see, hear, and feel, positive or negative.

# People in the puzzle

Place the people who influenced your childhood into the following illustration.

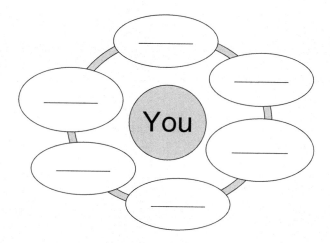

After putting the people into the circle, jot notes beside their name you believe important. You will use this illustration during the next series of discussion questions.

*Person 1* _____

Describe this person. _____

_____

_____

Describe the positive impact this person made on you. _____

_____

_____

Describe the negative impact this person made on you. _____

_____

_____

Discuss the emotions this person taught you how to express. _____

_____

_____

Discuss the emotions this person taught you to suppress. _____

_____

_____

What did you like about this relationship? _____

_____

_____

What did you dislike about this relationship? _____

_____

_____

_____

*Person 2* _____

Describe this person. _____

_____

_____

Describe the positive impact this person made on you. _____

_____

_____

Describe the negative impact this person made on you. _____

_____

_____

Discuss the emotions this person taught you how to express. _____

_____

_____

Discuss the emotions this person taught you to suppress. _____

What did you like about this relationship? _____

_____

_____

What did you dislike about this relationship? _____

_____

_____

_____

***Person 3*** _____

Describe this person. _____

_____

_____

Describe the positive impact this person made on you. _____

_____

_____

Describe the negative impact this person made on you. _____

_____

_____

Discuss the emotions this person taught you how to express. _____

_____

_____

Discuss the emotions this person taught you to suppress. _____

_____

_____

What did you like about this relationship? _____

_____

_____

What did you dislike about this relationship? _____

_____

_____

_____

*Person 4* _____

Describe this person. _____

_____

_____

Describe the positive impact this person made on you. _____

_____

_____

Describe the negative impact this person made on you. _____

_____

_____

Discuss the emotions this person taught you how to express. _____

_____

_____

Discuss the emotions this person taught you to suppress. _____

_____

_____

What did you like about this relationship? _____

_____

_____

What did you dislike about this relationship? _____

_____

_____

_____

*Person 5* _____

Describe this person. _____

_____

_____

Describe the positive impact this person made on you. _____

_____

_____

Describe the negative impact this person made on you. _____

_____

_____

Discuss the emotions this person taught you how to express. ____

_____

_____

Discuss the emotions this person taught you to suppress. _____

_____

_____

What did you like about this relationship? _____

_____

_____

What did you dislike about this relationship? _____

_____

_____

_____

*Person 6* _____

Describe this person. _____

_____

_____

Describe the positive impact this person made on you. _____

_____

_____

Describe the negative impact this person made on you. _____

_____

_____

Discuss the emotions this person taught you how to express. _____

_____

_____

Discuss the emotions this person taught you to suppress. _____

_____

_____

What did you like about this relationship? _____

_____

_____

What did you dislike about this relationship? _____

_____

_____

**Emotions**: We learn about emotions and how to express or suppress them most during childhood years. We learn the majority about emotions by seeing how the adults in our household handled their own emotions. It stands to reason that if those in our environment do not feel comfortable with their own emotions they cannot adequately equip us with that ability. Consider the most frequent emotions expressed and suppressed in your childhood environment.

Emotions are natural. A child expressing emotions can be frightening for parents who do not know how to express their own. Children being discouraged from expressing emotions, overtly or covertly, can become confused about their own emotions.

Here is an example: When a car hits a little boy's dog, he would naturally feel *sad*. A natural and healthy response to sadness would be *tears*. If one of his parents stopped the little boy from crying he would likely learn that sadness is not okay and eventually he may not express any emotions when he feels sad.

How might his emotions be stopped? A parent may say something to him like:

- Suck it up.
- Boys don't cry.

- Be a big boy.
- If you don't stop crying I will give you something to cry about.

The next time the little boy feels sad he might catch himself before he cries so he doesn't meet with disapproving parents. Doing this often enough would condition the little boy not to express sadness.

When this little boy grows into an adult, he may have difficulties in correctly identifying emotions expressed by others. This behavior can unconsciously translate into not even knowing how sadness feels.

This is only one example of how parents train their children to feel and express emotions.

Before we drill down into the history of our own emotions, first take a look at some basic material regarding emotions.

There is much debate among theorists about how many basic emotions exist. I will discuss them from my perspective. It seems there are only a few basic emotions and from them consist deeper versions.

> *All emotions are okay.*
> *Not all behaviors are.*

## Emotions categorized

In the column beside each emotion listed brainstorm as many degrees of that emotion you can think of.

| Emotions | Degrees of that Emotion |
| --- | --- |
| Exercise | I could be out of shape instead |
| Happiness | |
| Sadness | |
| Fear | |
| Anger | |

(continued)

| Emotions | Degrees of that Emotion |
|---|---|
| Exercise | I could be out of shape instead |
| Happiness | Enthusiastic  Ecstatic<br>Jovial  Joyful<br>Content  Peaceful |

All emotions are okay. Not all behaviors are. Learning to identify the feelings we are experiencing and giving ourselves permission to feel them can minimize inappropriate behaviors to follow. It is important to realize pain cannot always be avoided. If you want to experience the desired emotions fully you will have to allow the undesirable when they come.

Now that you have explored your own idea of emotions, it is time to drill into your emotional roots.

## A look back

In the right column, indicate your memories of how the emotion in the left column was handled by those surrounding you during your childhood. Consider if the emotion was comfortable, frequent, suppressed, frightening, or sought after. Feel free to jot about actual events where you recall situations related to the particular emotions.

| Emotion | How it was handled | Significant events recalled |
|---|---|---|
| Happiness | | |
| Sadness | | |
| Fear | | |
| Anger | | |

## Feelings

| Excited | Abandoned | Annoyed | Bored | Hesitant |
|---|---|---|---|---|
| Glad | Awful | Irritated | Distant | Rejected |
| Hateful | Afraid | Peaceful | Withdrawn | Loved |
| Calm | Hurt | Frustrated | Suspicious | Insecure |
| Proud | Vulnerable | Bugged | Anxious | Ashamed |
| Satisfied | Miserable | Uncomfortable | Disapproval | Optimistic |
| Embarrassed | Unloved | Furious | Confident | Disgusted |

| | | | | |
|---|---|---|---|---|
| Cheerful | Discouraged | Worried | Jealous | Moody |
| Relaxed | Lonely | Grumpy | Amazed | Satisfied |
| Content | Unhappy | Terrific | Mad | Violent |
| Surprised | Destructive | Confused | Skeptical | Responsible |
| Silly | Gloomy | Humiliated | Shy | Accepted |
| Delighted | Disappointed | Fuming | Mean | Destructive |
| Thankful | Sorry | Violated | Remorseful | Judgmental |
| Threatened | Scared | Sarcastic | Empty | Startled |
| Broken | Interested | Critical | Pessimistic | Isolated |
| Revolted | Repulsed | Indifferent | Apathetic | Mad |
| Furious | Powerful | Loving | Open | Inadequate |
| Ignored | Inspired | Victimized | Sensitive | Inferior |
| Infuriated | Hopeful | Alienated | Worthless | Submissive |
| Ridiculed | Disrespected | Powerless | Overwhelmed | Playful |
| Disapproving | Awe | Joyful | Intimate | Important |
| Avoiding | Despair | Desperate | Happy | Sad |

*In childhood we pick up on our environmental influences, simply by being there.*

What emotion would you consider was most frequently expressed by people in your childhood home?

_____

_____

What behaviors did you see as an expression of this emotion? _____

_____

_____

What emotion(s) would you consider were disallowed by people in your childhood home?

_____

_____

How did they let you know this emotion was not okay? _____

_____

_____

How was conflict dealt with in your childhood home? _____

_____

_____

_____

# Emotions today

Complete as it applies to your emotions today. Put an X in the appropriate box for how often you express the listed emotion.

| Emotion | Not enough | Sometimes | Enough | Too often |
|---|---|---|---|---|
| Happiness | | | | |
| Sadness | | | | |
| Fear | | | | |
| Anger | | | | |
| Other | | | | |

Looking back to the *Emotions today* chart discuss what holds you back from expressing emotions completely. ____

_____

_____

What are the payoffs and consequences of not expressing all emotions? _____

_____

_____

People adapt to their surroundings. The things you learned are historic. Knowing this information can further help you. It is your choice to decide if this information will enhance your future or be an obstacle.

# IMPACT OF HISTORIC EVENTS

Loss and trauma experienced as a young child makes a substantial impression for a lifetime, especially when those who surround you handle the experiences in a maladaptive manner. Of all the people I have worked with who report being sexually abused as children, those reporting the most long-term consequence are the ones who were not emotionally supported by adults. When a child is believed by adults and allowed to talk and work through the emotions of the trauma, they generally have a much better future outcome. Those children not believed who are discounted, silenced, and unsupported can experience a lifetime of pain and consequence from one or more traumatic event.

Adults with a history of unresolved loss and trauma would benefit from seeking counseling or support to work through this, so it does not negatively influence the rest of their lives. Having this information provides you the roots to the reasons you believe and behave as you do.

Once we know our history and reconcile unfinished business from the past, it is time to decide how the remainder of our life story will play out. To create a path to our goals we must first identify which of the historical events in our childhood we carried over to our current life and where they are having negative impact.

> *People are going to be who they are going to be. It is not my place in life to judge who they are or to attempt to mold them into whom I believe they should become.*

# Significant events

Discuss significant events having an impact on your childhood years.

| Event | Impact |
|---|---|
| *Example: My parents were divorced when I was 10* | *It hurt me a lot. It changed how I view love and commitment* |
| | |
| | |
| | |
| | |
| | |

# FAMILY RELATIONSHIPS

Important elements of relationships are trust, safety, and security. Discuss the meaning and impact of each of these words.

How do you define security? _____

_____

_____

How do you decide if you feel secure? _____

_____

_____

How do you define trust? _____

_____

_____

How do you decide to trust someone? _____

_____

_____

How do you define safety? _____

_____

_____

How do you decide if you feel safe with someone? _____

_____

_____

How are security and safety different to you? _____

_____

_____

How are security and safety similar to you? _____

_____

_____

Discuss any difficulty you might have expressing emotions to people close to you. _____

_____

_____

What keeps you from sharing how you feel? _____

_____

_____

How does the way others feel impact you? _____

_____

_____

What might cause you (or others) to stay in situations where you (or they) are unhappy? _____

_____

_____

What is your biggest fear? _____

_____

_____

What makes you feel safe and secure in a relationship today? _____

_____

_____

> *When you are used to being hurt, you will push people away*
> *—even those who really love you.*

## Security, trust, and safety

Under each column, place the names of people in your childhood you experienced security, trust, or safety with.

| Security | Trust | Safety |
| --- | --- | --- |
| | | |
| | | |
| | | |
| | | |
| | | |
| | | |
| | | |
| | | |
| | | |

For a moment look into how your security, trust and safety were formed.

How were your basic needs taken care of when you were growing up? _____

When you were afraid, how were you comforted? _____

Use the following activity to consider whom you trusted and reasons for the trust.

## Trust

| Who you trusted | What made you trust them? |
| --- | --- |
| | |
| | |
| | |
| | |

Discuss times people broke your trust during your childhood. _____

_____

_____

Do you trust someone until they prove to you they are not trustworthy or do you trust no one until they prove they are trustworthy? _____

_____

_____

# Developing trust

Discuss events during your childhood that reinforced your ability to trust or harmed your ability to trust.

In the boxes below, indicate the people you felt safe around when you were growing up.
Beside each person, indicate what made you feel safe with him or her.

## Safety

| Who made you feel safe? | How did they make you feel safe? |
|---|---|
| | |
| | |
| | |

(continued)

A few things to consider:

**Security** is another element of importance in relationships. Without essential needs being met one cannot feel secure. Without security it is not possible to grow emotionally into further vulnerability with the other person. While growing up you are dependent upon your family to meet these needs. Adults must create their own security.

Essential needs include:

- Food
- Clothing
- Shelter.

**Trust** is often viewed as black and white. You either trust someone or not. You may trust no one until they prove they can be trusted. You may trust everyone until they prove they cannot be trusted. Those are gut reactions based on experience. What if you shifted your definition of trust? What if you were able to look at trust as *recognizing consistent behavior?* Could that take some of the weight from your interpretation? A new definition I incorporated for trust is *being conscious of a person's behavior patterns and believing they will continue to follow that pattern.* I find this definition weight-lifting for many people. This definition could take the heavy emotion from the word trust. When intense emotions are minimized it is easier to view trust as more factual than emotionally loaded.

**Safety** is crucial in most relationships. When you do not feel safe in a relationship the intimacy is limited. When you continue to take risks with people who do not create a safe environment within your relationship you put yourself in jeopardy of being more deeply hurt.

Some of the things that damage safety are:

- Abuse
- Broken promises
- Infidelity
- Lies
- Fear
- Secrets divulged to others
- Inconsistency
- Control
- Manipulation.

Discuss times people made you feel unsafe. _____

_____

_____

How has safety played part in your adult life? _____

_____

_____

Describe the common conflicts you had in your family relationships during your childhood.

_____

_____

How was conflict generally resolved in your family relationships during your childhood?

_____

_____

What responsibility do you feel for unhealthy behaviors in family relationships during your childhood?

_____

_____

_____

What changes can you begin making in order to amend your relationships from childhood?

_____

_____

_____

What changes might need to take place for you to have more satisfying relationships with others? _____

_____

_____

*The way you spend your days is the way you spend your life.*

# Conscious Reflection

*Are you withholding love or approval because someone won't act the way you think they should?*

*What is your intention with that behavior?*

*Are you intentionally hurting them so they will suffer or do you even realize you are hurting them?*

# SOCIAL RELATIONSHIPS

List the friends you had growing up.

Beside each friend discuss how trust and safety were with that friend.

See the information following the activity for further instructions.

## Friendships

| Friends | Experience and outcomes |
|---|---|
|  | Trust:<br><br>Safety: |
|  | Trust:<br><br>Safety: |
|  | Trust:<br><br>Safety: |
|  | Trust:<br><br>Safety: |
|  | Trust:<br><br>Safety: |

*(continued)*

| | Trust: |
| | |
| | Safety: |
| | |
| | Trust: |
| | |
| | Safety: |

After listing the friends you had while growing up indicate the ones you were able to trust by circling "Trust" and those you felt safe with by circling "Safety" in each box.

Finish this activity by indicating in the blanks what caused you to feel or lack trust and safety with each friend.

## Current friendships

In your opinion, what are the characteristics of a quality friendship? _____

_____

_____

What changes need to take place for you to have more satisfying friendships? _____

_____

_____

Describe the common conflicts you have in your friendships. _____

_____

_____

How do you generally resolve conflict in your friendships? _____

_____

_____

What unhealthy behaviors have you been responsible for in past and current friendships? _____

_____

_____

What changes can you begin making in order to attain and maintain more quality friendships? _____

_____

_____

*We do not have to prove someone else wrong in order to be right.*

# Current romantic relationships

Romantic relationships tend to bring out our core issues more quickly than other interactions we have. That may be because of the level of risk and vulnerability is high in romantic relationships. When there are things we do not like about our romantic relationship it is futile to blame the other person. We are the only person we can change.

When we find ourselves saying things like:

*I wouldn't be rude if they weren't rude to me.*

*I said that to them because of what they said to me.*

What is the reason we continue to wait on the other person to change?

Sometimes people look into potential employment with more scrutiny than romantic relationships. Others avoid romantic relationships at all cost. Neither are healthy nor balanced approaches to romance.

What is your view of romantic relationships? _____

_____

_____

_____

What type(s) of romantic relationships did you witness while growing up? _____

_____

_____

_____

How have your adult romantic relationships been influenced by those you witnessed while growing up?

_____

_____

_____

_____

There are no particular number of or length to relationships to make them important and impacting. Like all other choices and behaviors, in order to attract more healthy romantic partners it benefits you to look at the patterns in your history. Beginning with the romantic relationship you are currently in—or the most recent—working backward, complete this activity as honestly as possible.

## Love life resume

| Person | Start/End Date | Strengths | Liabilities | Reason ended |
| --- | --- | --- | --- | --- |
|  |  |  |  |  |
|  |  |  |  |  |
|  |  |  |  |  |
|  |  |  |  |  |
|  |  |  |  |  |

# PATTERNS

Look over the dates in your *Love Life Resume*. Discuss patterns you are able to identify. *(Example: I noticed I do not end a relationship until I have secured another one. Most of my relationships begin within one month of the previous one ending.)*

_____

_____

_____

Continuing to look at the dates in your resume, what patterns can you identify regarding the average length of your relationships? _____

_____

_____

_____

What patterns can you identify regarding the reasons of your relationships ended? What pattern do you see in who ends the relationships most often (you or your partners)? _____

_____

_____

_____

What patterns can you identify regarding the characteristics of your relationships? Look at the strengths and liabilities. _____

_____

_____

_____

What impact do you see the examples of romantic relationships you had during your foundational years having on your romantic relationships? _____

_____

_____

What improvements could you make to have a healthier romantic relationship? _____

_____

_____

What insights have you identified about your romantic relationships? _____

_____

_____

Describe the common conflicts you have in your romantic relationships. _____

_____

_____

How do you generally resolve conflict in your romantic relationships? _____

_____

_____

What are your unhealthy behaviors in past romantic relationships? _____

_____

_____

_____

What changes can you begin making in order to attain more quality romantic relationships? _____

_____

_____

Discuss any behaviors you continue to hang onto but wish you could let go. _____

_____

_____

_____

What healthy characteristics do you desire in a romantic partner? _____

_____

_____

_____

From the characteristics you listed circle those you possess yourself. If you are not healthy it is unlikely you will attract a healthy partner.

I regret to mention that the most valuable lessons cannot be learned through stories but by experience. We cannot change simply by reading the words of another. It is often necessary to walk through our own story. Often that is painful. Recounting events that have been buried can hurt but the pain of living life on autopilot in order to avoid the digging is much more brutal.

Looking at patterns is the ultimate way to determine areas where change can take place. Often, we attract the same patterns in relationships. Only when we see what those are can we change the things about ourselves that continue attracting negative relationships or continue doing the things that attract positive relationships.

If you want to make major improvements in a current romantic relationship, I challenge you to ask the other person today:

*What is it like to be in a relationship with me?*

If you do not have a great deal of intimate conversation in the relationship, this can be a scary question to both parties. If you are afraid to hear the answer to such a question, ask yourself the reason.

As you review events from your earliest years consider advice you wish you had been given or had taken when you were a teenager. If you, as an adult, could offer advice to yourself as a teenager, what would you say?

## Advice to my teenage self

## Examining your support system

In order for each of us to be healthy, aware, and making positive progress toward our goals, we need a healthy support system. A healthy support system consists of people who:

- Encourage us
- Are honest with us
- Share hard to hear advice with us
- Do not abuse or abandon us
- Give as much as they take.

*Who we surround ourselves with predict the outcome of our future.*

Take a closer look at the people who surround you and what they contribute.

Place the names of people surrounding you in the circles.

Indicate those who meet the criteria of being part of a healthy support system by drawing a **straight line** to and from you to them.

Indicate those who do not meet the criteria of being part of a healthy support system by drawing a **curved line** to and from you to them.

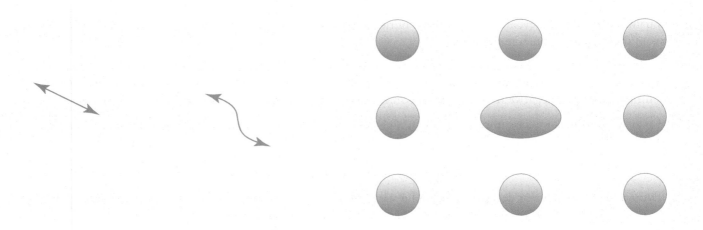

# BOUNDARIES

Boundaries keep you safe. If you have healthy boundaries you will find a balance between staying safe and taking calculated risks. There is a difference between healthy boundaries and putting up walls. Walls keep people out and are often a sign of fear.

- No one can force you to do anything.
- Surround yourself with people who support, motivate, and challenge you.
- Own your story. No one can use your story against you when you are at peace with yourself.

Do you keep your promises to others? _____

What is the reason? _____

_____

_____

Do you keep your promises to yourself? _____

What is the reason? _____

_____

_____

How does it feel when others let you down? _____

_____

_____

How does it feel when you let others down? _____

_____

_____

Who do you blame when things go wrong for you? _____

What is the reason? _____

_____

_____

Using the boundary activity, discuss with whom you currently have working boundaries and what these boundaries protect you from. This can give you a quality example of how you might implement them with others.

## Current boundaries

| Person | Boundary | Protects you from what? |
| --- | --- | --- |
| Example: John | I do not loan him money. I have told him this and have stuck to my word since I told him | John used to borrow money and never pay it back. Not loaning him money now protects me from not being paid back |
| | | |
| | | |
| | | |
| | | |
| | | |

With whom do you need to set boundaries? Also discuss reasons you have not done so at this time. _____

_____

_____

What is the best and worst thing that could happen if you set these boundaries? _____

_____

_____

Keep in mind, when setting boundaries people who have been violating them will not be pleased. They may even attempt to blame you or make you feel bad for taking care of yourself.

In addition to setting boundaries with others, it is important we set them with ourselves. We cannot live in drive. Once in a while we need to slow down. I hear from people daily:

*I am so tired.*
*I just need a break.*
*I have too much to do to think of taking any time for myself.*

Taking time out for us is paramount to our success. Once we become burned out, even when we keep working, we are not giving our best. When we are not giving our best, we are slowing the progress to our goals. We do not need money or a lengthy vacation to focus our energies inward. We simply need to give our care daily priority. Take 2–5 minutes to yourself each day. We all waste more than that each day. Here are a few ways I, and others I know, spend time to reenergize on a daily basis.

- Five minutes each morning before getting my children up, I drink coffee and look out the window at my lawn focusing on all the blessings in my life.
- I use an upbeat, energizing ring tone for my wake-up alarm.
- I write positive messages to myself on my mirror so it is the first thing I see when I awaken.
- After my alarm rings, I lie in bed a few moments focusing on positive thoughts.
- As I drive to work each day I turn on my "theme song" and sing along—very loudly.
- Each evening, when the house gets quiet, I spend two minutes with a daily reading in a meditation book. Even if I have to lock myself in the bathroom for privacy, I make sure I get those two minutes of "me time."
- I take my dog for a walk around the block every night before I go to bed. It is good for both of us.
- Instead of working through lunch at my desk, I walk around my office building a few times. It helps get to be away from the environment and clears my head.

## THE DREAM

If your life could look exactly as you wish, how would it look? Be as detailed about the changes as possible. _____

_____

_____

_____

_____

What makes the change you picked an ideal situation to you? _____

_____

_____

_____

_____

What obstacles need to be removed from your current life to have the life of your dream?

_____

_____

_____

_____

What would the worst-case scenario for your life be? _____

_____

_____

What would the best-case scenario for your life be? _____

_____

_____

# Life of your dreams

In the activity box, list the way you dream your life to become. List all of the characteristics, emotions, activities, and details of the life of your dreams.

# The reality of life

After duplicating the dream list, to the right, complete a list of all the characteristics, emotions, activities, and details of the life of reality of your life.

| Life of your dreams | Reality of your life |
| --- | --- |
| | |

# The obstacles

Examine the reason you are not living the life of your dreams. In the center column enter the obstacles that stand in the way of the life of your dreams.

| Life of your dream | Obstacles | Reality of your life |
| --- | --- | --- |
| | | |

# Finding excuses

Circle all of the obstacles that are real, and not imagined.

Draw a square around the obstacles that are real and can be overcome with work.

Draw one line through the obstacles that are not real, those imagined, or used as excuses.

What is the reason you allow the imagined obstacles to keep you from the life of your dreams? _____

_____

_____

Discuss the payoff for hanging onto behaviors that no longer work, keep you from your dreams, or keep you stuck? _____

_____

_____

Many times when asked the reason they are not living the life of their dreams, people reply, "money." I think that is an easy way out. Unless money falls from the heavens into your lap are you going to live the rest of your life wishing and blaming? Do not give into that excuse.

There will be an excuse for everything we do not like in life if we look for one. If you have a bad relationship with your mother you can blame her for the person you are and the results you are getting in life today. Continuing to blame your mother allows you to remain the same and not take responsibility for your change.

## What or who do you blame?

Taking control of the obstacles will allow you to make the changes to get the dreams you want from life. To live the life of your dreams it is important to examine what you are and what you are not in control of.

## Control

Review the lists with your dreams, obstacles, and current life. Dissect the areas you do and do not have control.

| Areas you have control | Areas with limited control | Areas with no control |
| --- | --- | --- |
| | | |

# MAPPING THE COURSE

Finding your purpose in life starts with looking at some of the following questions:

What fulfills you? _____

_____

_____

_____

_____

If money were not an issue, what would you do for work? _____

_____

_____

_____

Anyone can dream of a successful future. Not everyone achieves the goals they set for themselves. What will make the difference for you? How will you reach your goals?

_____

_____

_____

_____

What do you want to leave as your legacy? _____

_____

_____

_____

What are you willing to sacrifice for your dreams/goals? _____

_____

_____

_____

# Thought stopping

To remove the obstacles that are imagined, it is important to stop the negative thoughts that create the imagined obstacles.

## Stay conscious

- Remain in the present with your thoughts.
- Focus on today.
- Stay focused on today, not in the negative events from your past.

## Block your internal bully

- From time to time those negative thoughts and old stories will sneak in.
- Do not entertain the thoughts when they do pop up.
- Do not allow yourself to play the story through.
- Take charge of your thoughts.

## Reaffirm

- Daily remind yourself of your goals, your value, and your ability to accomplish the goals.
- Wake up with positive thoughts.
- Consider the positives in your life.
- Do not focus on the negative, unless you are considering the things you have control of changing.

## Commitment to your dreams

What if I told you that your dream life can become reality, no magic wand required? I believe most dreams can become reality when the obstacles are removed and we put action behind the wish. There are many reasons people in their mid-life who have had a dream their entire life still have that as a dream but not a reality. If you want to accomplish the things you say you want, take a few steps past wishing.

While building your dreams before turning them into goals, take a few steps:

- **Affirm your worth**

  Before you can make any dream come true you have to believe you have enough value to attain the dream.

- **Imagine yourself living the dream**

  Close your eyes and see yourself as if the dream is already true.

  Use vision boards by pasting photos, words, or articles that spell out your dream.

  Place these in spaces you see them daily so they are continually in sight.

- **Eliminate the obstacles**

  Those things you allow to get in the way of living your purpose must be eliminated. Some of these are real, many are imagined, but each must be eliminated.

  Making your dreams come true takes a few steps, the last the most critical.

- **Stay committed**

  With the dream in mind daily, stay committed to seeing it through to the end.

- **Map it out**

  Take a realistic look at what it takes to accomplish this dream.

  Set goal(s).

  Break the goal(s) down into steps.

- **Take daily action**

  To accomplish a goal you must work toward the goal, daily.

  This is one of the most important of all the steps.

  You will not wake up one year from today with a goal having been obtained by

  osmosis because you wish it so.

  Dreams take sacrifice.

Hard work cannot continue without an occasional break. Allow a bit of time for yourself. Find a peaceful space in your home or outdoors for two or three minutes each day to simply organize your thoughts and focus on your purpose. Living each day with intention will get you closer to your dreams in a shorter amount of time.

# List the goals you want to have accomplished *one year* from today.

**List the specific steps it takes to meet the goal.**

**List the daily steps it will take to meet this goal.**

**List the goals you want to have accomplished *five years* from today.**

**List the specific steps it takes to meet the goal.**

**List the daily steps it will take to meet this goal.**

**List the goals you want to have accomplished *ten years* from today.**

## List the specific steps it takes to meet the goal.

## List the daily steps it will take to meet this goal.

Are you willing to make the daily sacrifices to meet your goals? _____

The commitment to the sacrifice is to you, and not anyone else.

Similar to the advice you wrote to yourself as a teenager in previous activities, make a commitment to accomplish your goals through writing a promise to yourself dated 10 years into the future.

## Commitment to my future self

# COMMUNICATION

We communicate daily with the world around us, even if we are not aware. Not speaking, body language, tone of voice, and eye contact, or lack thereof, sends a message. If we want to have a more positive impact on others and feel better ourselves, it is important to begin paying more attention to what we are communicating. Following the workbook section there will be more information about healthy and effective communication.

How well do you believe you communicate? _____

_____

_____

How did people communicate with you as you were growing up? _____

_____

_____

How did your family communicate with one another while you were growing up? _____

_____

_____

With whom do you feel most comfortable communicating? _____

_____

_____

What does this person do to make them easy to communicate with? _____

_____

_____

What are the obstacles standing in your way of communicating in the most effective way possible? _____

_____

_____

# Your inner voice

Many people repeat messages to themselves they have heard from others all of their lives. These can be positive or negative messages. The messages you repeat over and over in your own head are reinforced and become your truth. It is important to be conscious about the messages you repeat to yourself.

Take a look at the messages you continue to reinforce to yourself about yourself.

# Repeated messages

Imagine you are going to a job interview. As you walk toward the door of the company, what are you saying to yourself over and over about the interview? _____

_____

_____

_____

Imagine you are getting out of your car to head inside the coffee shop to meet a potential romantic partner for a blind date. As you walk toward the door of the coffee shop, what are you saying to yourself over and over about the date? _____

_____

_____

_____

Imagine you are headed into the door to take a final exam for a test you did not study for that will determine if you pass or fail the course. What are you saying to yourself over and over about the test? _____

_____

_____

_____

Messages repeated over and over—to yourself or out loud to others—come from somewhere. If you want to stop negative messages you are repeating to yourself or to someone else it is important to know the origins of those messages.

# Origins of the voice

In this activity, first list messages you find yourself repeating. The second step is to determine if the message is positive or negative. Finally, to connect the dots from today with the past, decide where you learned or heard each message.

| Message | Positive or negative? | Who told you this? |
| --- | --- | --- |
| | | |
| | | |
| | | |
| | | |
| | | |
| | | |
| | | |

# Non-verbal communication

Much of our communication is without words. It is important to be conscious about verbal and non-verbal communication.

Consider how you communicate thoughts and feelings, in certain circumstances, by indicating your non-verbal actions in the box to the right of the feeling or situation presented.

| Feeling/Situation | Non-verbal actions you use to communicate your response |
| --- | --- |
| *Example: Anger* | *I slam doors and sigh loudly* |
| Anger | |
| Happiness | |
| Sadness | |
| Frustration | |
| Loneliness | |
| Fear | |
| When rejected | |
| When congratulated | |
| When corrected | |
| When lied to | |

People use non-verbal communication for various reasons. Many of our hand gestures and facial expressions are learned. Many people are not even aware of how they look when they communicate. If you want to have an eye-opening experience, have someone video-record you while you are speaking. You may see yourself in a different way when you view the recording. Non-verbal communication is both positive and negative. Examples of non-verbal behavior include the following:

- Sighs
- Red face
- Eye rolling
- Clenched fists
- Smiling or smirking
- Covering face with hands
- Looking down, up, or away from the other person
- Any behavior inconsistent with what is being verbally communicated.

What are the reasons you communicate in the non-verbal ways you do? _____

_____

_____

How might you improve your communication? _____

_____

_____

What might change in your life if you improved your communication skills? _____

_____

_____

_____

What keeps you from verbally communicating instead of relying on non-verbal communication to express yourself? _____

_____

_____

Like everything you have considered throughout this workbook, communication is a learned skill and can be relearned to be more effective.

**Notes**

_____

_____

_____

_____

_____

_____

_____

_____

_____

_____

_____

_____

_____

_____

_____

_____

**Notes**

# Communication

*Listening, not talking, is the key to communicating that far too many people miss.*

# COMMUNICATION

In Section 2, we will cover communication in more depth. We will explore:

- Motives for communication
- Obstacles to effective communication
- Conscious communication
- Audience
- Tips for effective communication
- Skills of effective communication.

## Motives for communication

What are the reasons we communicate? When I have asked this question, I have heard various answers.

- To get my point across
- To prove my point

91

- To express my wants
- To express my needs
- To share my emotions
- To share information
- To get information.
- To influence or convince others
- To connect
- To pass time
- To control others
- To vent
- To receive communication back.

If we begin to communicate for the following reasons we are likely going to hit a brick wall:

- On principle
- From anger
- To be right
- Out of fear
- To control or manipulate.

*No one can read your mind. Words are necessary.*

# Obstacles to effective communication

Many things can get in our way of communicating effectively. You spent a great deal of time during the first section of *Living in Consciousness* identifying many personal obstacles. Here are some common obstacles to many people:

- Distrust
- Dishonesty
- Distractions
- Resentment
- Stereotyping
- Defensiveness
- Lack of time
- Failing to listen
- Hidden agendas
- Casting judgment
- Different perceptions
- Offensive hand gestures
- Tone or volume of voice
- Using your opinion as fact
- Failing to ask for clarification
- Wrong or disruptive atmosphere
- Non-verbal and verbal not matching
- Written instead of verbal communication

- Allowing your history to influence what you hear
- Wanting to be right or prove the other person wrong
- Using words or language the other person does not understand.

# Conscious communication

Examining the reason for each communication is important. Often communication is without consciousness. When we engage before thinking about our intention it can end poorly. This is especially important when the communication is significant and not casual conversation. Before we communicate it would payoff to consider:

- What makes this important?
- What do I hope to gain by saying or doing this?
- How likely is it that I will get what I hope to gain by saying or doing this?
- Has saying or doing this worked for me in the past?
- Is there a better alternative?
- Is the other person ready?
- Is this a good time?
- Is it best to communicate this message in person or in writing?

The more we live consciously and aware of our beliefs, behaviors, and the connection between the events that occur today to the triggers in our history, the more we are able to avoid unintended conflict. Being aware of what you want to communicate and picking the best words to use, time to begin, and method to use, the better the outcome.

# Audience

Who we are communicating with or to plays a role in how we communicate. If there is no difference between the ways in which you speak to your child than to your boss, it might be time to reconsider the effectiveness of your skills. Here are some things to consider about your audience:

*Social*: When talking with friends we can be relaxed, friendly and use common jargon. In communication with friends we are able to let down our guard and speak from the heart a bit more. This is an informal level of communication. It is appropriate to have equal give and take in our interactions. These relationships are most healthy when they consist of trust, safety, and security.

*Intimate:* Intimacy does not always mean a sexual relationship. Sexual relationships without intimacy occur all the time. Intimacy is a level of sharing that requires safety, trust, and security that leads to a willingness to be vulnerable. Each person contributes sharing and support of the other at an equal level. What we share and how you communicate depends on the relationship and is negotiated between the two parties as the relationship develops. It is within intimate relationships some of our deepest growth is possible. This is also a level of informal communication.

*Professional*: This is a formal level of communication. While we may be friendly with people we are speaking with, there are still professional norms we need to stay aware of. Our boundaries are more rigid when communicating professionally. The words we chose are more formal. Making presentations, emailing, and phone calls are part of professional communication.

- It is inappropriate to use profanity.
- When sending professional emails we need to use formal wording. It is inappropriate to email your professor or supervisor using the same greetings and rhythm as you would use with a friend.
- When speaking with customers or clients on the telephone, we may be friendly, but must keep appropriate boundaries and respect, acknowledging the type of relationship.

With all audiences, it is important to:

- Listen and be attentive to the other person speaking.
- Remain present in the conversation.

# Tips when interviewing someone

Communication connects us with others. In order to connect in the way we intend, it is important that we communicate well. You have spent a great deal of time becoming more aware of how your history can be an obstacle in your communication. Remember, not everyone has done this work. Keep in mind when you are communicating with others, they too, have a history through which they filter what they hear and say.

The following are a few important tips that can help achieve the best results:

## Be prepared

Prepare for interactions, especially when the conversation will be difficult. Don't take the spontaneity out of interactions but do consider the intention before getting started.

## Connect

Human nature causes us to look for something familiar in others. Connect with those with whom you communicate, but do not forget to allow them to be who they are, as well.

## Silence is therapeutic

Silence can be uncomfortable but it is necessary and actually helpful. Become comfortable with silence between you and the other person.

## Empathy

Understanding must be authentic and genuine. Empathy cannot be fake without coming across as phony. It is important to truly care.

## Be clear

Do not ramble or mumble. Listeners will soon stop listening if they have to strain to understand the message.

## Be kind

Being direct does not mean being tact-free. Kindness goes a long way when communicating. It is possible to say what we mean or be firm while being kind.

## Be short and sweet

In formal situations or when interviewing someone, it is important to allow the person you are interviewing to do most of the talking.

## Listen to learn

Be genuinely interested in what is being said. Allow the other person to share their story. Do not interrupt them or finish their sentences. No matter how well we know the other person, listen with the intention of learning something new.

## Allow the person to answer

When we ask someone a question, allow him or her to give an answer. Do not interrupt, finish their sentences, or appear disinterested.

# Have the courage to say what you mean when you have hard to have conversations

At times we may need to share something that is difficult. These are important conversations to have, no matter how uncomfortable. Consider how you will say what you need to say and attempt to do so without negative emotions overtaking the conversation.

# Ask for what you want

People cannot read our minds. Tactfully tell others what you want and need.

# Ask the other person what they want

When unsure what the other person is communicating, ask them to clarify.

# Consider the vocabulary

Not everyone understands the way we speak. Consider the other person when selecting the words to use.

# Practice

Anyone new to conducting professional interviews or are not used to open communication will benefit from practice.

# Eye contact

Looking at people when we speak is important. Do not forget to use appropriate eye contact.

# Offering feedback

When people close to us are in difficult situations ask for permission to give them feedback. People are more likely to be open to hearing us when we have their permission.

# Body language

Be aware of what you are saying through body language.

# Use appropriate volume

Ensure the person you are talking to can hear. Also make sure you aren't speaking so loudly such that they disengage or perceive you as aggressive.

# Be kind

No matter what type of communication, personal, professional, or even in a check-out line, be kind to people.

# Support

When attempting to support another person during a difficult time, we often struggle for what to say. Sometimes simply asking the person how you can support them is enough.

# Use a strainer

- Not everything you think needs to be said.
- Do not speak out of negative emotions.
- Think through your motives when your feelings take over.
- When caught off guard, take a breath.

- Things said cannot be taken back. Something said in 30 seconds can take years to heal.
- A child can be broken by a parent's words. The continual use of destructive words can tear them down.
- Build people up with your words instead of tearing them down.

# Avoid

## Do not ask "why"

Asking "why" seems to cause people to be defensive. There are so many ways to ask why without using the word. Review the discussion questions in the workbook area for examples of various ways to ask questions without beginning with why.

## Do not take hostages

Be aware of social cues. Conversations come to a natural conclusion. Allow them to end.

## Do not fix

Unless someone asks for it directly, do not give advice. Often people simply want to vent or talk something through.

## Do not have expectations

Having expectations of others will let you down. Others do not know what you expect unless you communicate your wishes to them. Do not expect another person to behave in the same way as you.

## Do not talk too much

Communication is as much about listening as it is about talking. Allow people to answer questions and tell their story.

## Do not judge

When we judge the person we are talking with we limit the interaction. We hear only what we expect and the judgment becomes an unseen obstacle for both parties.

## Do not assume

When we think we know what the other person means, we stop listening. When we assume we know what they are going to say next, we stop listening. When we assume we are hearing the other person through our own experience, we are not listening to their story.

## Do not discount

When the problem another person has is not something we would consider a problem, it is tempting to discount their problem by telling them something worse that we are going through. Do not discount the gravity of another person's journey. We cannot know what the struggle is like for them; we can only accept what they share as the truth.

## Do not interrogate

Closed questions can sound like an interrogation. Instead of using 20 closed questions, the story is often found in asking two or three quality open questions. An interrogation sounds like this:

Mary: What would you like to discuss today, Steve?

Steve: I am so tired after work; I just want to sit on the sofa and watch television. I don't have any energy anymore.

Mary: Have you changed your diet recently?

Steve: No.

Mary: Do you exercise?

Steve: Not that much.

Mary: Are you drinking enough water every day?

Steve: I guess so.

Mary: Have you tried vitamins?

Steve: No.

Mary: You should try vitamins.

Steve:

Do you get my point? A more effective way to respond to Steve would have been:

Mary: What would you like to discuss today, Steve?

Steve: I am so tired after work; I just want to sit on the sofa and watch television. I don't have any energy anymore.

Mary: Tell me what you think is causing you to be so tired, Steve.

This allows Steve to explore his own solutions and tell you the story. This first example is exhausting for both people.

# Skills

When conducting professional interviews, the words we use, attentiveness, and our listening skills are important.

# Explain

Inform the person you are interviewing the purpose of your interview.

# Open questions

Open questions allow the person being interviewed to go into as much detail as they care to. Open questions cannot be answered in only one or two words.

Below is an example of how to turn a closed question into an open one:

*Closed*: *Were you raised in Texas?*

*Open*: *Tell me about where you were raised.*

*Closed*: *Do you enjoy your job?*

*Open*: *What are the things you enjoy about your job?*

# Curiosity

Ask questions in a curious way. Come from a place of genuinely wanting to know more about the person being interviewed.

# Reaffirm

Restate what you hear the person saying once in a while to confirm them you are listening.

# Connect statements

When someone mentions a situation more than once in the same interview or conversation, consider connecting the statements together. This will confirm you are listening. It will also help tie thoughts together for them.

# Digging in

Stay present and aware in order to use your intuition to know when the person being interviewed is ready for you to ask deeper questions.

# Confirmed interpretation

Asking the person if what you understood them to say is actually what they meant.

An example might be: So, Tom, I think what I am hearing you say is you are having trouble with your new boss. Is that right?

# Encouragement

Use verbal and non-verbal cues to encourage the person to continue sharing.

Below is an example of both:

*Verbal: Using encouragers like yes, umm, and I understand is often all you need to say to reassure the person to continue sharing.*

*Non-Verbal: Nodding your head, as the person shares will often help reinforce that you are listening.*

# Normalize

When the person being interviewed seems embarrassed by what they share, use statements to normalize what they are sharing to assure them you are not judging them.

Below is an example:

*Feel free to share anything you would like.*

*Nothing you say changes my opinion of you.*

*I can see how that would be difficult.*

# Advice to helping professionals

In addiction courses or when supervising new counselors, I offer this advice. I believe it applies to many other professions, as well:

- Listen more than you speak
- Complete documentation on time and as an accurate historical account of your/the client's work
- Ask more open than closed questions
- Deal with your own issues outside of work
- Work is about the client, not you
- You will always be entitled to your opinion. But opinions are not fact
- Your journey does not define the map for your client
- Learn how to write professional letters and email
- Respond with respect to your supervisors
- Effectively communicate with clients, co-workers and supervisors
- Take responsibility
- Seek supervision. The only stupid questions are the ones you don't ask
- Take care of yourself. You cannot help anyone if you have not helped yourself
- Ask for help
- Use humor
- Have your own support system
- Don't burn bridges. You have only one reputation
- Let the client tell you their story

# 3. Interviews

*One of the most valuable possessions another can give is their time. Respect that gift.*

## INTERVIEWS

Several people were generous enough to share their time and stories with me. This allows me to provide examples of how others benefited from working through the workbook. I also provide examples of the interview transcripts labeled with the Communication Skills used.

## Dusty

Dusty is a university student in recovery from addiction. He is employed in the addiction recovery profession.

**PHG**: Thank you for meeting with me and allowing me to record our interview. As I explained when I asked you to meet me, this interview is a series of questions about your childhood that I will be using in the second edition of *Living in Consciousness*. Feel free to answer any questions you feel comfortable. *{Explaining the purpose of interview}*

**Dusty**: No problem. You can ask anything. I am an open book.

**PHG**: Describe to me the place you call home. *{Open question}*

**Dusty:** That is kind of interesting because I don't really call anywhere home. I was born in Arlington, Texas and my first memories were living on a small farm in Fort Worth. My mom and I moved away from my father when I was fairly young and we moved quite a bit, actually. I don't really call anywhere home. When people ask where I am from I just say DFW.

**PHG:** Okay.

**Dusty:** My early memories were pretty good. We had pigs, chickens, and a Shetland pony. Everything started out Southern-American, picturesque. But it didn't end up that way.

**PHG:** Awe . . . *{Encouragement}*

**Dusty:** We moved from the farm to Fort Worth. My mom didn't have any education so we moved into a battered woman's shelter over in a not so great part of Fort Worth. My mom ended up becoming a pseudo-counselor there . . .so she took on a job there . . .and I went to stay with my Grandma. That was around kindergarten. I stayed with her a little while but that didn't work out so well because she had some issues. She was a recovering alcoholic but after she stopped drinking she started abusing diet pills so she had some meltdowns and that didn't work out too well.

**PHG:** Mmm hmm . . ..*{Encouragement}*

**Dusty:** I went back to live with mom. That was about the time she had my little brother. She was working, like, three jobs with a baby. She was working at the shelter and waiting tables and I was going to Catholic school at the time. I didn't see my mom too often because she was always working and I had babysitters who lived by the school. Mom drove a bus, so I would get picked up on the high school bus. She had teenage girls and that was cool.

**PHG:** That is interesting.

**Dusty:** My memories are very compartmentalized to the man my mom was dating at the time. She would have a boyfriend for several years, then her next relationship would last a number of years. So that is how my memories are associated.

**PHG:** mmm hmmm, these are the "Jim" years. These are the "Tom" years? *{Confirming interpretation}*

**Dusty:** Yeah, yeah. Because, they were all so different, you know? And it was all based on—because my mom has always been a sweet lady—but our lifestyle was definitely dictated by whom she was dating.

**PHG:** Okay, okay . . .that makes sense. I understand that. *{Normalizing}* So, what are some things you liked about your childhood years? *{Open question}*

**Dusty:** I lived in several areas where we had horses, cattle, living out in the country. I didn't care for the shelter or Catholic school because we were poor. I got into a lot of fights so I transitioned into public school in Irving, Texas. That was about the time my mom met Tommy. He was an alcoholic neighbor, a construction worker. We moved out to Argyle on about 15 acres.

**PHG:** Oh, how cool.

**Dusty:** There were good parts and bad parts. Of course, he was an alcoholic, but we had horses and dirt bikes. We also got to shoot guns all the time. Not a lot of safety but at the same time I learned a lot that I wouldn't have learned otherwise. I got to drive tractors. It was good for me. It wasn't always good for our neighbor. We shot pellet guns at each other. Someone always got hurt. But in the background it was always dysfunctional.

**PHG:** Uh huh?

**Dusty:** Tommy had a stepson, Devon. We had a lot of conflict and that led to conflict with me and Tommy. It was me, my brother and Devon. It was me against him and Tommy. That caused a lot of physical conflict. When there was physical conflict between me and Tommy my mom would leave. Actually, it was the end of her last relationship, too. She would leave. Once I didn't like you, I was going to get rid of you one way or another. I think I was thinking to myself, "if you aren't smart enough to get rid of this looser, I will get rid of him for you."

**PHG**: Were you identifying things wrong with the men that your mom couldn't see or did you just not like anyone your mom dated? *{Digging in}*

**Dusty**: I had a picture in my mind of what I wanted a stepdad to be like. Have a normal job, not get drunk and smoke weed all the time. Not smack me around and cuss all the time. I wanted to live in a nice normal neighborhood in a certain kind of house. I had a way I thought things should be.

**PHG**: Right . . .(nodding)

**Dusty**: And, I knew that was not the way things were supposed to be. Oddly enough, we kept going through that cycle. Later Tommy and my mom reconciled right after I started junior high in Denton. I was always a good student. I was in student council. I was a very focused kid, did all the normal things. I was a social kid. I hadn't been corrupted yet. (Laughing)

**PHG**: (Laughing)

**Dusty**: It was cool, living on a much larger ranch and my dad started coming around again. I think because my dad sold Tommy drugs. My dad had a job at General Motors but broke his back and he started using pain pills and transitioned from prescriptions to illegal drugs. My mom left him because he kept having girlfriends. They were always much younger girlfriends. He had this one girlfriend who used drugs and he ended up getting into drug dealing.

**PHG**: mmm hmmm (nodding head)

**Dusty**: But there were good times, too. We had fun. There were always people out there. But at the same time, there was always an undertow of violence. Tommy would get drunk and we would fight. He was a grown man, a Vietnam Vet, he had served some prison time and I was not afraid to call him out on anything that I didn't like. So, it got back to where it used to be. I don't think I realized the danger I was putting myself in back then. We moved to The Colony after the whole head of cattle caught tuberculosis and had to be put down.

**PHG**: Oh, wow.

**Dusty**: My mom was exposed to therapy and AA—because my grandmother was in AA—she kept trying to get Tommy into therapy and rehab. He finally went into rehab reluctantly and when he got he had a fairly decent attitude. But, it wasn't long until he relapsed. But, my mom got into that and took hold of therapy quite a bit and started doing the work on herself. When he came out and was doing what he was supposed to do she supported him but when he relapsed she did everything she was supposed to.

**PHG**: mmm hmm

**Dusty**: We went to stay with my mom's sponsor and Tommy quickly disappeared. I found out later that Devon went to prison for 14 years . . .

**PHG**: Wow.

**Dusty**: Tommy is still alive and Devon and I communicate through Facebook now. He has straightened his life up so kudos to him. Anyway, after that it was just me and my mom and my brother again. I guess I was about 13 then. That was a turning point for me. I got curious about everything then. I suppose I identify The Colony as home for me, really.

**PHG**: I see . . .

**Dusty**: I guess I skipped a big part of elementary. My mom dated another man back then. I didn't get along with his son. When we would get into fights he would tell us to go in the backyard and fight until someone bled. He was really screwed up. His son wouldn't want to. He would hang onto to the door trying to stay inside and his dad would make him go outside and fight me. Another guy she dated went to prison. My mom stuck with him. In retrospect, I understand more about victim blaming. Everything he ever did wrong he blamed on someone else. I didn't understand this then but inherently I knew something was wrong with doing that.

**PHG**: Right, right.

**Dusty:** My mom continued on with therapy but she didn't really believe there was any evil in this world. She allowed people to blame their childhood for things they did wrong. I was 13 years old. I got drunk a couple of times so my mom sent me to rehab. I didn't need it at that time but everyone told me I was alcoholic in there so I got out and lived up to their expectations. I still did well in school after I got out. There were relatively no consequences except for a lot of fights. That was a real turning point. It went from just experimenting with drugs to getting deeply involved.

**PHG:** That is a lot.

**Dusty:** Around 15 years old I went into rehab again. I got into a situation with a lot of friends. There were weapons, an assault, a bunch of trouble. My friends ran and got away. I didn't. I was taken to juvenile. Fortunately, I was released into my mom's custody and back into a rehab. I never disliked being in rehab. Even then I was such a knucklehead. I got out and it did plant a seed. I knew I couldn't continue to live that way. I got back involved in church and the youth group.

**PHG:** Many of the men in your life have had some strong characteristics. From them, what have you carried into your adult life? *{Curiosity}*

**Dusty:** Resentment mostly.

**PHG:** What behaviors?

**Dusty:** I have my father's womanizing characteristics. I can be violent, when I was using. I have a mean streak. It isn't the same now but when I was drinking. A lot of bad things I never would have thought. I was just like my father for a while with the drugs, guns, violence, and women. Mom finally met a good guy named Al and that was about the time I met Nikki. Al was such a fantastic human being and they were together about 15 years before he died with cancer. I never really excelled in anything because I didn't have anyone to guide me.

**PHG:** mmm hmm . . . .

**Dusty:** My mom and I have always had such a bond. She was really young when she had me so she talked to me about a lot all of my life. We all leaned on each other and I knew a lot about how she was raised. Our relationship wasn't real traditional. It was just us against the world.

**PHG:** I was wondering, since your mom sought counseling, you were in rehab and now seeking education to be a counselor, what kind of conversations you have with her today. *{Connect statements}*

**Dusty:** Eventually, we talked about all those things. For a couple of years, there was nothing she could say about it. One day she finally told me she understood but I couldn't keep using that as an excuse for my adult decisions. We are pretty close now and very open about everything. There is nothing uncovered or not dealt with. Fortunately, we have aired our dirty laundry. I think my life would not have been as bad if I had a little more guidance.

**PHG:** Thinking back on your mom's life, what do you think it was like to have been your mother as a child?

**Dusty:** That is probably the reason I understand and forgive her so much now. My mom and her sister coped with so much in their childhood. They had a sister who died and had an alcoholic mother who was in and out of sanitariums. My uncles went off to college and excelled in academics. They left their sisters to fend for themselves. Her dad did some really questionable things and her grandfather was a pretty horrible man. That was my mom's growing up so I understand she wanted to get away from that as soon as she could. The person my mom turned out to be was pretty excellent given that she didn't have any guidance. It was probably a lot worse than my mom has even told me.

**PHG:** Many of her choices make perfect sense given her history. *{Normalizing}*

**Dusty:** Absolutely. I think my brother and I are the ones who have been able to finally break the cycle.

**PHG:** You have given me so much information. I really appreciate your time and story.

**Dusty:** No problem. I hope I gave you something good to use.

# Leigh

Leigh is a 30-year-old professional who was interested in working *Living in Consciousness*. She volunteered to answer questions to be used in the workbook.

**PHG**: Thank you for meeting with me today. I will be asking you a few questions to get to know you better. Feel free to stop me at any time or ask for clarification if you ever need. *{**Explaining the purpose of the interview**}*

**Leigh**: You're welcome. I am glad to be here.

**PHG**: Good. I am thrilled to hear you are glad to be here. *{Reaffirming}* Let's get started!

**Leigh**: I am ready.

**PHG**: Tell me how you describe yourself to someone you are meeting for the first time. *{Open question}*

**Leigh**: I am loyal. I am a hard worker. I communicate well. I am a family man. I enjoy spending time at home more than being out. I am confident. I stay positive and friendly. Should I keep going?

**PHG**: I am enjoying hearing about you. Share as much as you want. *{Encouraging}*

**Leigh**: I have weaknesses, too.

**PHG**: (Nodding head) I think we all do. *{Encouraging and normalizing}*

**Leigh**: I am sometimes impatient. I don't like to wait. If I go to a grocery store and there are more than three people ahead of me in line I will leave. I know I need to work on that.

**PHG**: You need to work on being impatient? *{Reaffirming and curiosity}*

**Leigh**: I do.

**PHG**: How does being impatient impact your life? *{Digging in}*

**Leigh**: Well, like the grocery store, I leave without the grocery I need. I think my temper is too quick so waiting is hard.

**PHG**: Tell me about your temper. *{Digging in}*

**Leigh**: I am not proud of it. (Hangs head)

**PHG**: It's okay. I am curious to hear all about you, the good *and* the bad. *{Non-judgmental}*

# About the author

Paula Heller Garland has been an addiction professional since 1993. Her work as a clinician has included counseling and administration in a myriad of settings and populations: residential, in-prison, outpatient, those with HIV, and criminal justice.

As immediate past president of the Texas Association of Addiction Professionals (TAAP), Paula's main focus has been on advocacy, growing membership that includes more students and interns, and bridging the gap between prevention, treatment, and recovery.

She is a Senior Lecturer at The University of North Texas (UNT) in the Department of Disability and Addiction Rehabilitation where she values the opportunity to teach and mentor, future counselors. At UNT, Paula serves as the Coordinator of the Addiction Program, Clinical Advisor of the Collegiate Recovery Program, and Faculty Sponsor to students in the Eagle Peer Recovery Organization.

Paula enjoys conducting workshops for other helping professionals, traveling, writing, her dachshund Max, and spending time with her family.

#Livinginconsciousness

Facebook: https://www.facebook.com/LivingInConsciousness/

Twitter: @LivingNConsciousness

CPSIA information can be obtained
at www.ICGtesting.com
Printed in the USA
LVOW01s1107130816

499784LV00002B/2/P